CHRISTMAS STORIES OF LOVE AND HOPE

Cathy A. Weaver

TEACH Services, Inc.
P U B L I S H I N G
www.TEACHServices.com • (800) 367-1844

Copyright © 2022 Cathy A. Weaver
Copyright © 2022 TEACH Services, Inc.
ISBN-13: 978-1-4796-1483-7 (Paperback)
ISBN-13: 978-1-4796-1484-4 (ePub)
Library of Congress Control Number: 2022906258

The stories in this book are based on true experiences. Most names have been changed. Characters' thoughts, feelings, and actions may be author's perceptions only.

Any similarities between the reader and a character bearing the reader's name are purely coincidental.

Published by

TEACH Services, Inc.
P U B L I S H I N G
www.TEACHServices.com • (800) 367-1844

Dedication

This book is dedicated with gratefulness
to my heavenly Father, whose amazing
love gave us the first Christmas—
the One who daily renews our strength, forgives
our sins and mistakes, heals us, restores us,
and, incredibly, brings good out of life's most painful moments

Table of Contents

Acknowledgements

With special thanks:

To my loved husband and best friend, Dave, who endured a not-so-clean house and sometimes late, boring suppers, who patiently listened to me read each story (more than once) and gave me encouragement and good suggestions. Without his support, this book could not have been written.

To my precious daughters who are a joy to me, and who give me much love and encouragement even though I made many mistakes as a mother. They are truly my friends.

To my sons-in-law, who made a lifetime commitment to my daughters, and whom I love as sons.

To my beloved grandsons and granddaughters, who love me even though I don't really know how to be a grandma. But I'm learning!

To my beloved brothers, whose faith and love for God has influenced and inspired me. They regaled me with family stories, encouraged me to write, and were helpful reviewers.

To my one and only very special sis, who is always forgiving, cheerful, and encouraging.

To my cherished youngest brother, who was there for me during a most painful time in my life, and who gave me ideas for another book. His love brightens my days.

To my dear little mother, Orphia, who would be so pleased and proud that I am finally using my talents. How I miss her!

To dear Howard, who provided the computer and Microsoft® Word program, and who has always done everything he could to facilitate my writing.

To Deb, my busy teacher friend, who spent hours reviewing my stories and making corrections and suggestions. I could never pay her what she is really worth.

To my treasured friends, Sue and Jazmin, who believed in me, encouraged me to use the talent God gave me, and prayed for me. Sue told me to keep a small notepad with me at all times for ideas.

To Karen at Pacific Press Publishing Association, who had a part in my healing, whose stories inspired me to write my own, and who encouraged me and gave me helpful information.

To my high school English teacher Mrs. Vardon, who recognized and encouraged my talent and taught me how to write better. I will never forget her.

To Aunt Phyllis Roark, who enjoyed my Christmas letters and urged me to write a book. She advised me to keep a notebook of ideas for every project that came to mind. She planned to help me get a book published, but unfortunately, she passed away before she could be part of this.

To Joe L. Wheeler, whose *Christmas in My Heart* series has brought me much enjoyment and need of tissue boxes, and who loves to mentor young and old. I had the privilege of sitting in Gem State Academy's English class twice when he came to mentor students.

To Dr. Smoake at New Mexico Institute of Mining and Technology.

To my boss and friend, Beth, who reviewed my first manuscript and saw something I hadn't seen.

To Josué, who writes beautiful poetry and stories, and encouraged me to keep writing.

To Pam and Bill, who reviewed several of my stories and gave me hugs and positive words.

To Dan and Sue, my great neighbors, for their help and encouragement.

To Ann and Marie, who assisted me with kind words and a list of publishers.

To my parents, for passing on the writing genes.

To John, for making this venture possible.

To Timothy and his excellent publishing team at TEACH Services Inc.

And to the men and women, too numerous to name, whose lives inspired me to become a better person.

Last but not least, a very special thank you to our heavenly Father, who gave me the ideas and words, and without whose help I never could have written this book. Time and again after reading through a story I had just written, I shook my head with amazement and tears, because I knew it wasn't me who had done it. God had come through for me, yet again.

Christmas Eve

Lord, on this special night,
As I imagine Joseph and Mary's
Journey on a donkey
Underneath a dark sky
Brilliant with stars,
I hold my breath
With excitement and wonder
In anticipation of the miracle
About to be.
Love, born in a stable!
Infinite God in infant flesh!
Newborn hope in a manger!
Bright angels herald the joy
To shepherds tending their flocks.

With the angels I burst into song—
Glory to God!
Glory to God in the highest!
Sin's bonds slip away,
My soul thrills
With peace and good will,
And I cry with the shepherds,
Oh, come, let us adore Him!
Cathy Weaver, January 4, 2014

A Christmas Epiphany*

"Mom, when is Dad coming home?" I questioned as I dried the last dish and put it away.

"I'm not sure. He hasn't called yet." Mother's brow furrowed with worry. "Would you help me get the little ones to bed?" she asked.

Ignoring the nagging uneasiness in my mind, I helped my little sister wash up and get into her pajamas. Connie and Jerry cuddled up to me while I read them a Christmas story. Mother came to hear their prayers and tuck them in.

"Your father has an alcohol problem," she rasped. "That's why he's been coming home late for the past couple of months."

"Goodnight, Muffin! Good night, Bug! I love you!" I sang as I slipped out of the room and hurried downstairs. Pushing aside the living room curtain, I peered out into the darkness. Snowflakes were falling rapidly past the shining streetlight. "I hope Dad didn't get into an accident," I murmured to myself.

"Susan, I need to talk to you." I jumped at Mother's gruff voice. My heart began to pound.

What did I do wrong? Is she going to yell at me and beat me like last time? Warily I turned and faced her. I wasn't sure how to interpret the look on her face.

"Your father has an alcohol problem," she rasped. "That's why he's been coming home late for the past couple of months. I..." Her voice broke. "I have no idea where he is or when he will be home." Her lips trembled.

---

* Epiphany—when you suddenly see or understand something very clearly, or in a new way.

"I don't want the little ones to know. Please help me keep it from them. Don't tell anyone. You're fourteen now and old enough to keep a secret."

Stunned, I nodded my head. Then I fled to my room, horrified, yet relieved. My shocked mind seemed to dash in a hundred directions as I sank onto the bed.

So that's why he hasn't been coming home for supper. I wish Pete was here instead of away at school. I don't know what to do, I panicked. *What do I do, God? What's going to happen to us?* A sudden thought came to me.

Maybe Dad wasn't on a business trip last month when Mother said he was. When he finally came home, she had to help him walk up the stairs. She said he was sick, and we couldn't see him until morning. Maybe that terrible smell in his room was alcohol, not garlic.

Oh, Mother must be beside herself with anxiety, especially with snow coming down. Poor Mother! I do love her even if she does treat me wrong sometimes. She must really be hurting if she confided in me when we haven't even been getting along.

Softly, I tiptoed back to the living room. Mother sat in the armchair by the Christmas tree, staring into space. Impulsively, I went behind the chair and hugged her around the neck, my head on her hair. Mother patted my arm gently. Then she jumped up.

"I have no idea where he is or when he will be home."

"I might as well do my exercises while I'm waiting." She got down on the floor and started doing leg raises.

I watched for a moment. Then I got down on the floor and exercised with her. Together we worked in silence, listening for a car. When we finished, Mother turned out the lights, but she didn't go to bed. She sat waiting in the darkness. I waited with her. She didn't say a word.

Finally, around eleven o'clock Mother spoke. "You'd better get to bed. You have school tomorrow." She was still up when I fell asleep.

The next morning when Mother came to wake me, she whispered, "Your father didn't come home. There's a check missing from the back of the checkbook and he'll probably be gone until his money runs out. Remember, don't say anything."

Dad was gone for a week. I overheard Mother on the phone telling his boss that Dad had the flu. We made excuses to our family and friends. I felt embarrassed and ashamed.

Finally, Mother received a call, but it wasn't Dad. It was the police. Dad had fallen asleep while driving drunk, and had crashed his car into a highway bridge. He had survived, with only cuts and bruises. Mother put me in charge and left for the emergency room.

Dad ended up losing his job, and Mom began looking for work. By the time Pete came home for Christmas break, I just had to tell someone. I was astonished when Pete said he knew that Dad had a drinking problem. Well, if Pete already knew, maybe Mother wouldn't be too upset if she found out I told.

Christmas Eve arrived. *Merry Christmas,* I thought, cynically. *Very merry, with Dad's alcohol problem and no job, and probably no presents. And Mom going out to work soon. How am I supposed to manage the house and the kids by myself? Mom has been nicer to me since the night I stayed up with her, but with all these stresses who knows when she will get angry and beat on me again?*

My cynicism dissolved into desperation as a sob rose in my throat. *Oh, God, I can't do this! Are you really there, God? Do you care?*

After the children were in bed, I asked Mother if I could sleep on the sofa so I could look at the Christmas tree. I could hardly believe it when she said yes. She never let anyone sleep on the sofa except Dad.

Pete was on a date and Mom and Dad went to bed early. I got my pillow and blanket and turned the radio on low so no one would hear it. I relaxed into my pillow, basking in the quiet beauty of the tree. Pete's red-and-white-robed choir boy and my blue-robed angel stood on opposite branches, close against the trunk. As always, I pretended I was the angel and imagined what it was like to be up in the tree looking out through a fairyland of colored lights and shining ornaments.

Abruptly, a carol I had never heard before caught my attention. It sang of winds blowing through olive trees in Bethlehem long ago, and angels singing to shepherds watching their sheep.

Afterward came a song that spoke of the night wind and a little lamb, and a star dancing in the sky. A shepherd boy told a mighty king about a little Child shivering in the cold, a Child who would bring us goodness and light.

As I gazed at the nativity scene beneath the branches of the Christmas tree, I thought about that little baby in the manger. I began to imagine Mary and Joseph's journey by donkey. All of a sudden, it seemed I was in Bethlehem. I felt the night wind blowing through the olive trees and playing with my hair as I walked the dusty street. I witnessed Joseph and Mary's arrival, too late to get a room at the inn. In the stable a cow mooed a soft welcome to the exhausted couple, while a small kitten purred and kneaded fresh hay in the manger. I heard a newborn's cry, and contented sighs as his tiny stomach filled with warm milk.

Out on the hillside, shepherds huddled around a campfire, keeping watch over their sleeping flocks. Suddenly they froze with fear as an angel appeared—like a lightning bolt—with a startling announcement of a baby, a Savior, lying in a manger. An angel choir burst into rapturous song, lighting up the sky from horizon to horizon. With the shepherds, I ran to the stable where we stood in silent awe adoring the baby. Into the reverent stillness intruded the sound of heavy, plodding feet and men's commanding voices. Through the open doorway, by the light of a blazing star, I beheld three majestic kings dismounting from kneeling camels. Entering the stable, the kings knelt and offered their gifts of gold, frankincense, and myrrh, worshipping the baby King.

Then I remembered why Jesus came as a baby, and I worshipped, too. And I knew that He saw me, that He *always* sees me! He *is* goodness and light. He takes away sin and sadness.

In that moment, my heart felt strangely comforted, even joyful! My problems had not vanished, but I knew He was with me, giving me strength. I knew I would make it through, because He came. Because He loved me enough to be born in a smelly stable, and to live and die for me.

That was a turning point in my life. Very slowly things began to improve in our home. I became Mother's right-hand helper and we grew very close. Dad stopped getting drunk and eventually he gave his life to Jesus.

Life is still a struggle at times, but I know I'm not alone. I know I'm loved. Because every Christmas, when I hear "Winds Through the Olive Trees" and "Do You Hear What I Hear?" I remember. I remember the night God reached down to a scared, lonely, confused teen, and made Christmas come alive.

The Crushed Bicycle

What am I supposed to do about Christmas? It's only two weeks away! I've got to have a little Christmas for my girls. Please, God, I begged silently as I followed Natalia and Candy up the street to the playground. Since Thanksgiving, this had been my heart's cry. Outwardly I was the usual cheerful mom, making paper snowflakes with my girls and decorating the apartment with greens and Christmas candles, but inwardly I was pleading.

You know it's impossible with only $2.00 left after paying bills. You've got to help us! You're our only hope.

Candy parked her bike outside the gate and raced over to the slide with her big sister. We had the playground to ourselves, as usual.

Well, at least she finally has a bicycle, I thought. *That's one good thing.* Aunt Bonnie and Uncle Mike had rescued the discarded bicycle from the dump and repaired it. They had sanded it and painted it a lovely pale yellow in time for Candy's seventh birthday, and she loved it.

I pushed my burdens aside and gleefully began playing with the girls as though I was a kid again myself.

A while later I glanced outside the fence where the yellow bicycle ... had stood. Oh, no! Someone *stole* it? In *this* neighborhood?

I dashed over to the gate and outside the fence. There in the dead leaves lay the yellow bicycle, mangled beyond repair. Appalled, I glanced around. A trailer truck was backed up to the loading dock across the driveway. Huge tire indentations in the leaves led directly to the yellow bicycle.

Oh, God, I can't believe this! She's only had it for a month! Why didn't we bring it inside the fence? Why didn't I look up when I heard the beep, beep, beep of the truck?

Cautioning the girls to stay inside the playground, I reluctantly dragged myself toward the bookstore and the dreaded confrontation. Just inside the door, Gary, the manager, was working on a book display.

There in the dead leaves lay the yellow bicycle, mangled beyond repair. Appalled, I glanced around.

"Is the truck driver in here—the one who just ran over my daughter's bicycle that she got for her birthday?" I asked him. Gary pointed to a burly man in a black leather jacket a couple of aisles over.

As I timidly approached the man, he scowled at me. "Excuse me, sir," I began bravely. "You ran over my daughter's bicycle."

"Well, what do you want *me* to do about it?" he snarled. "That's not my problem, that's your problem." Abruptly he turned away.

Tears stung my eyes, but I held my head proudly until I got around the end of the aisle. Then I ducked my head and pretended to examine books until the words no longer blurred.

Oh, God! I thought I was done with harsh words when Jeffrey left us. Why did he have to be so mean? I didn't do anything wrong. What do I do? No Christmas, and now no bicycle. Be my Champion, Lord. Fight for me!

Surreptitiously I peeked over the top of the book display. A couple of aisles away, the manager was talking to the truck driver. I lowered my head and picked up another book.

There's nothing else I can do, Lord. It's up to You.

A minute later I felt a tap on my shoulder. Turning, I cringed to see the truck driver beside me. But no sharp words came from his mouth. Instead, he kept clearing his throat.

"Uh … I'm sorry about the bicycle," he growled. "Here!" He pressed something into my hand. "It's all I have."

I opened my hand. In it was a $50 bill. My heart leaped! Speechless, I gaped up at him.

"It's all I have," he insisted defensively.

A smile broke over my face. "Oh, thank you, sir! Thank you! God bless you!" The driver cleared his throat again and marched out the door without looking back.

Gary came over to me. "Did he give you anything?"

"He gave me $50!" I exclaimed. "He apologized."

"Good, he better have. I talked to him a little."

"Thank you, Gary! This is an answer to my prayers."

My heart nearly burst with joy as I ran back across the driveway to the playground. *Christmas! We can have Christmas! You are an awesome God! You are amazing! I will love you forever!*

Glory in His Eyes

"Gilbert, I think I will lie down. I am very uncomfortable." Elzaida spoke quietly, rubbing her abdomen with both hands.

Gilbert smiled understandingly at his wife. "I hope you can get some rest," he replied. "I will put the children to bed. Then I'll be in to check on you." He listened to her heavy footsteps retreat down the hall and into the bedroom.

Fortunately, the winter nights brought him home from the woods early. Elzaida's mother, who usually helped with the children, was enjoying an early Christmas with Elzaida's sister Marion in California. Gilbert glanced at the calendar. The baby was not due until Christmas, the doctor had said. "Mou" would return to New England in plenty of time.

Gilbert gave his namesake a bath first. Little Gilbert, otherwise known as Bunny, splashed and played with a rubber duck as Gilbert scrubbed his skin pink. Wrapping him in a towel, Gilbert carried him to his bed and dressed him in a clean diaper and pajamas. He lifted the crib rail into place, then made Bunny a bottle of warm milk. Bunny stood up and reached for it. Leaning down, Gilbert kissed his soft, clean hair, breathing in his fragrance.

"Let's talk to Jesus," Gilbert said. Bunny dropped his bottle and put his small hands together. He repeated after Gilbert as best he could.

"Dear Jesus ..." Gilbert paused to let Bunny lisp the words with his baby lips. "Please ... take care ... of Mama ... and Daddy ... and Mou ... and Jack ... and Tiny ... and Bruzzy ... and Jake ... and Chubbins ... and Punky ... and Godey ... and Bunny ... Amen."

Gilbert gave him a hug, and Bunny plopped a milky kiss on Gilbert's cheek. "Good night, Bunny. I love you," Gilbert said.

"Wuv oo," Bunny gurgled. He lay down and popped his bottle back into his mouth. Gilbert handed him his special blankie and covered him up.

Next, three-year-old Godey, their only girl, was tucked into her crib in Bunny's room. Punky, five, and Chubbins, seven, were big boys who didn't need much help. Jake and Bruzz were staying at the schoolteacher's house in town for the month of December. It was a good thing they were there tonight, with the snowstorm raging outside. The shrieking wind threatened to tear the wooden shutters off the farmhouse.

Tiny went to bed next, upstairs in the large front room where Punky and Chubbins were already asleep. Fifteen-year-old Jack was the last to go. He chose to sleep year-round on the screened porch. Jack had become quite a strong young man, in more than one sense of the word. Gilbert could depend on him.

After checking on Elzaida, Gilbert stood at the boys' door listening to their even breathing. He pushed the door open a little so he could see their tousled heads in the light from the hall. How he loved them! *Help me be a good father,* he prayed. Down the hall, he crept in and gently removed the glass bottle from Bunny's bed and pulled up the blankets. If Elzaida did not feel up to it, he would check on these two later in the night and make sure they were still covered. They slept so soundly they would never know they were cold until they awoke shivering and crying.

Back downstairs, Gilbert looked in on Elzaida and saw that she was asleep. *Good.* His dear one needed her rest, kept busy as she was by her little brood, and carrying a new life within her.

Soundlessly he closed the bedroom door, then opened the solid oak door into the large front entryway. He peered out the front door of the farmhouse and watched the snow come down. There must be a foot already, and the wind was piling it into drifts. He was glad the baby wasn't due yet. No one would want to go out on a night like this.

Gilbert left the entryway, closing the door tightly behind him, and pulled on his boots, coat, and cap. Quietly he went through the house and out the back door, being careful not to let the wind grab the door from him. Fighting his way across the drifted driveway, he entered the barn and drew from their hiding place the wooden toys he was building for Christmas gifts. He worked on them for a while, but the raw cold numbed his fingers, and he restored the toys to their hiding place. Going inside, he sat before the oil stove and warmed himself, thinking how blessed he was to have a good wife and family. Oh, they were a trial at times, but those were opportunities for him to exercise patience. He wouldn't trade his family for anything. Sometimes it was difficult to keep food on the table for so many, but God always provided. They had never gone without.

The warmth of the stove made him drowsy. Logging was heavy work, but he loved it. Out in the woods a man was his own boss. Alone with the deer and the foxes, a man had time to think, to feel the peace of the woods lighten the burden on his back. It was easy to talk with God out there in the stillness while tramping through the forest, selecting a tree. He reveled in the earthy smell of the forest, the growl of the chain saw, the ability to land a tree exactly where he wanted it, the strength of his arms as he rolled the logs with a peavey to his waiting truck. Yes, a man was a man, in the woods. He knew every tree by its bark and shape. When cut, each variety of tree had an odor all its own, the sugar maples kind of sweet, the black oak tempting him to check his shoes for dog manure. Lately, he had taken Jack with him, and Jack's sharp mind had quickly memorized the Latin names and the differences between the trees. He was a good companion, and worked as well as any man.

Smiling to himself, he recalled a late summer evening when he had worked overtime. He had greeted his wife lovingly and put away his hat. By then the younger children, fortified by naps and still awake, had tumbled down the stairs crying, "Daddy's home! Daddy's home!" He had gotten down on one knee and they ran into his arms, each carrying a worn stuffed animal or toy for him to see and touch. Their fervent love had warmed his heart and dispelled his weariness. They should have been in bed, but inwardly he had been pleased when his wife had set plates at the table for them. Eagerly they ate with him the rhubarb they had refused at supper, while Elzaida sat watching them, a half-smile on her face. Afterward he had carried them piggyback up to their beds.

The grandfather clock chimed nine o'clock. Gilbert got up and turned down the oil stove. Then he made his rounds, making sure everything and everyone was safe for the night. Before he got into bed, he knelt.

Father, thank you for the good day. Forgive me for my sins and mistakes. Lord, I ask that You please watch over us tonight in this storm. Watch over Bruzz and Jake, and the teacher and his family. Watch over Mou and Marion and her family, and bring Mou safely back to us, I pray. I ask in Jesus' name.

He slid under the covers carefully, so as not to wake Elzaida. It seemed as though he had been asleep for only a moment when he vaguely became aware of something tugging at his arm. Was he dreaming? From far away, someone was calling his name.

"Gilbert, wake up! Gilbert!" Why, that was Elzaida's voice. Instantly alert, he sprang from the bed. The baby was coming, on this stormy night!

Reassuring Elzaida, Gilbert ran out to the porch to awaken Jack.

"Jack, the baby is coming early. I need you to hurry over to the Fords' house and ask to use their telephone to call Dr. Hallock. Dress warmly. You should be able to tell where the edges of the road are, even in this storm. Come right back; I may need your help." Jack had seen kittens and calves being born. He would be all right.

Jack, already in his clothes and wool cap, jumped up and pulled on his boots. Gilbert hurried back to the bedroom. Sending up a prayer for wisdom, he assisted his wife as well as he could. At least he had been present at six of their babies' births, so he had a pretty good idea of what to expect. He wondered how long it would take the doctor to drive the twelve miles in the storm.

It seemed as if it took an hour for Jack to battle through the blizzard the quarter mile to their nearest neighbor's house and back.

"The doctor said he will come right up," Jack assured Gilbert. "I sure hope he can get through—some of those drifts were pretty high when I waded through them."

The contractions were coming closer together now, and Gilbert wondered if the doctor would arrive in time. Elzaida's babies came fairly quickly, and Gilbert did not see how it could be much longer. He turned as Elzaida groaned.

"Jack, dash out to the kitchen and put some water on to boil, and bring me some clean towels and washcloths. It looks like the baby will get here before the doctor does."

Gilbert's hands trembled with excitement. After all, how many fathers get to deliver their own baby? He steadied himself. Birth was a normal part of life. He had delivered calves before; this couldn't be that much different. He rolled up his sleeves and washed his arms and hands well. Sending up a quick prayer, he rushed to Elzaida's side.

Lord, it's you and me. You've never failed me, and I know you won't fail me now.

He didn't. Frank James was born without complications, with Gilbert and Jack presiding. Gilbert was unaware that his little flock, awakened by the commotion, waited halfway up the darkened stairs. Jack discovered them, silhouetted by the starred wallpaper, when he darted out to the kitchen to grab the steaming kettle. "The baby's coming!" he exclaimed. The waiting siblings whispered and hugged each other with excitement. When little Frankie lay clean and dressed in his mother's arms, Gilbert called them in, one at a time, to greet their new baby brother. Each one left the bedroom with shining eyes, a reflection of the glory in their father's eyes.

Loud banging on the front door startled them. Striding through the cold entryway, Gilbert threw open the door. A snowman stood outside, but the blue eyes above the snow-covered face scarf seemed strangely familiar.

"Terry, come in! What made you struggle through this storm?" Gilbert asked his neighbor.

"Dr. Hallock called. He tried three different ways to get here, but the hills are just too slippery. He said you have seen enough births and he's certain you can do it yourself. He will be over tomorrow as soon as he can get through."

"Thank you, Terry. The doctor was right. But I didn't do it by myself. I had Jack and the Lord helping me. Come and see our little Frankie!"

The next morning the storm was over, but the country road remained impassable. Gilbert waded through the snow to Terry's house to call Jake and Bruzz, who were elated to hear of their new baby brother. Mou drew in her breath with surprise when he called her, and Dr. Hallock was relieved to hear that the birth had gone well, and that mother and newborn were all right.

"The road has not been plowed and my truck is out of commission," Gilbert told him, "but I have an idea. If you can get to the bottom of the hill, Jack will be there at ten o'clock to bring you the rest of the way."

Back at home, Gilbert instructed Jack to unbolt the saw from the Model A coupe cut-down chassis they had been using as a sawmill. Jack wrapped Gilbert's logging chains around the rear wheels. Climbing up to the seat, he drove down the hill to meet the doctor. Afterward, Jack grinned as he told Gilbert that Dr. Hallock had raised an eyebrow at the strange mode of transportation.

"But he handed his doctor's bag to me and climbed up. He held the bag on his lap and seemed to enjoy his ride out in the open," Jack chuckled.

After examining Elzaida and the baby thoroughly, Dr. Hallock clapped Gilbert on the shoulder approvingly.

"Well done," he exclaimed. "I couldn't have done better myself."

Late on Christmas Eve the sound of a hammer came from the barn. The children and Mou were asleep when Gilbert finally carried in the tree and trimmed it. He fetched the toys and other handmade gifts and arranged them under and around the tree. Elzaida filled the children's stockings with goodies and added her presents to the tree. Content at last, they knelt to pray before crawling wearily into bed. Christmas morning was sure to come too soon.

During the night Gilbert was awakened by little Frankie's stirring. Slipping out of bed, he tiptoed over to the bassinet and lifted Frankie's warm, snuggly body to his shoulder. In a few seconds Frankie quieted down, so Gilbert made his way out to the warmth of the stove. Holding the sleeping baby in his arms, he gazed into the face of the new son God had given him. What a miracle he was! Many a night Gilbert had sat in front of the stove holding a new baby, and he had never yet wanted to send one back. Each baby was a miracle. Each baby was unique, beautiful, loved. His throat swelled with gratefulness and pride. Thinking of the difficulties of life, he longed to shield Frankie from all danger and heartache.

Lord, bless this son that You have given us. Protect him and help him grow into the man You want him to be.

> God must have longed to protect His newborn Son and shield him from danger and heartache, just as I do.

The oil flame sputtered as a gust of wind blew down the chimney. The grandfather clock ticked quietly.

I am holding my newborn son in my arms just as Joseph held the Christ Child on that starry night so many years ago, Gilbert mused. *I wonder if he felt like I do. Actually, baby Jesus was God's own Son. Why, God must have longed to protect His newborn Son and shield him from danger and heartache, just as I do. He must have yearned to watch him grow into the man He wanted him to be. Did He, like me, bend low to gaze lovingly into his Son's face, realizing what a miracle he was? For all births are miracles—the births of kittens and calves, the birth of a child—even the birth of a world. Surely God looks, with glory in His eyes, at what He has created, and takes joy in how beautiful it is. Surely He feels that way about every one of us, for He is our heavenly Father.*

The grandfather clock chimed the quarter hour. Little Frankie awoke and fussed. His flailing fist accidentally touched his mouth, and he began sucking on it. Gilbert stood up and carried him to his mama's waiting arms.

A Christmas Surprise

"Amma! Let's go exploring!" Robert called as they got out of the car. "We could see hundreds of interesting things before Mom gets out of her appointment!"

"All right, but Robert and Joshua, remember to stay with me and don't touch anything," his grandma replied.

Together they walked up the street, keeping watch for something fun to explore. Turning the corner, Robert peered through a glass door into a gift shop. He saw birdhouses and statues and all kinds of gifts.

"Amma! Can we go in here? Please?"

"Yes, just remember the rules," Amma reminded them. Robert pushed the door open, and Joshua and Amma followed him inside.

"Hello!" A lady smiled from behind the counter. "Enjoy yourselves and look around. Here we have hot chocolate, lemonade, caramel popcorn, and other snacks. Upstairs we have a Christmas shop."

They looked at each other, grinning.

"Let's go upstairs!" Joshua led the way. At the top of the stairs they paused and looked around.

"Ooh! A Christmas village! Look at the train!" Robert's voice rang with pleasure. The boys watched the train chug around and around, past the village, beside the frozen pond, through a tunnel in the mountain, and back past the town again. Christmas lights decorated the buildings and Christmas trees. Tiny people stood on the snow and skated on the pond.

After a time, Amma spoke. "I'm hungry. It's almost lunchtime. Anybody want a snack?"

"I do!" "I do!" The boys scurried down the stairs. The three of them shared a bag of caramel popcorn.

"That was fun, Amma! Where can we go now?" Joshua asked. "I know! Let's go to the train museum!"

"Yes!" agreed Robert. "I love trains! I hope they have the caboose open. I've never been in the caboose."

"We don't have enough time to go through the museum," objected Amma. "But we could walk down the street and see if the caboose is open," she suggested. "I doubt if it will be, in the winter, but at least we could look through the fence."

They walked back down the street to the bottom of the hill. As they crossed the wide road, Robert looked through the fence at the huge caboose sitting on a track in the yard.

"Oh-h-h, the caboose isn't open. There's a padlock on the door." He sounded very disappointed.

They walked back up the street to the car, and soon Mother was done with her appointment. On the drive home, they told her about their fun time exploring.

A few days later, Amma said to Grandpa Dave, "Robert has no school on Thursday. He loves trains so much, and he has never been in the caboose. Let's take him to the train museum! We can take Joshua another time when he is out of school."

Thursday arrived, and soon Amma, Robert, and Grandpa Dave were headed for the train museum. Grandpa parked the car and they crossed the street.

"Oh-h-h," Robert groaned. "The caboose isn't open today, either. I'll never get to go."

"Don't lose hope," replied Amma, "God loves to give us the desires of our hearts when we delight ourselves in Him."

They walked up the steps and entered the old train station museum. Grandpa Dave gave money to the lady behind the ticket window, and they began exploring the museum.

In one room they saw a model of the big hotel that used to sit on Main Street, and a phonograph that Thomas Edison had invented. Amma especially enjoyed some old-fashioned ladies' dresses and a wedding gown. In another room they found old tools, wringer washing machines, and antique corn huskers. "There's an antique corn sheller just like my grandpa had," Grandpa Dave told them. "It takes the kernels off the cobs."

Finally, they reached the best room of all—the train room! On its walls hung old lanterns and other train equipment from long ago. At a little store they could buy train hats and toys. In a glass case in the middle of the room, model trains puffed around a track and through a tunnel whenever someone put money into a slot.

Robert, Amma, and Grandpa Dave looked at every item in the train room. Then Amma gave Robert a quarter to put into the slot to make the model trains run. They watched the trains chug across the bridge, through the countryside, past the silver mine, and into the mountain tunnel. Last of all, Amma bought a train whistle from the gray-haired man behind the counter. He wore a striped train hat and striped overalls, and looked very much like a train engineer.

"Don't lose hope," replied Amma, "God loves to give us the desires of our hearts when we delight ourselves in Him."

As the man pushed down on tall buttons on an old silver cash register and put their money into it, he asked Robert, "Would you like to explore the caboose?"

"Uh, what?" questioned Robert, not sure he had heard correctly.

"Would you like to go see the caboose?" repeated the engineer.

"Yes!" Robert nearly danced with excitement.

"Okay, let's go!" The man put on his coat, picked up a ring of keys, told the ticket lady where he was going, and led the way outside to the fence. He unlocked the gate and they all followed him to the caboose and waited in the snow while he unlocked the padlock. Stepping aside, he motioned for them to climb up.

"Go ahead. Enjoy!"

Robert and Amma quickly climbed up into the caboose. Inside, the upper walls and ceilings were painted light green. Robert pretended to warm his hands at a potbelly stove that stood in the corner close to a long bench. A small table stood next to a bench on the other wall. He hurried through a short hallway into a second room.

As Amma walked through the hallway, she noticed there were drawers and closet doors in the walls. "This must be where the trainmen kept their clothes," she thought aloud. "Or maybe the food and dishes." When she entered the other room, Robert grinned up at her from a bed covered with an Army blanket.

"Get up!" Amma scolded, laughing. "You don't work on this train!"

As they crossed back through the hallway, Amma showed Robert the closets.

"Hey!" Robert exclaimed. "What are these metal bars for? It looks like a ladder. And there are some on the other wall, too!"

"That's where the trainmen climbed up so they could look out the windows and see the whole train and everything around it," the engineer spoke as he came in with Grandpa Dave.

"See the platforms up above? Go ahead and climb up," he said.

Robert and Amma climbed up the ladders to the platforms and looked out the windows. They could see in every direction.

"I can see the whole train!" Amma pretended. "There's a tunnel up ahead."

"I can see where we've been," imagined Robert. "There's a herd of buffalo crossing the tracks behind us."

After they climbed down, they rested on the long benches while the train engineer explained what it was like to be a trainman years ago. Suddenly, a train screeched along one of the many tracks behind the museum. They rushed to the door to watch it go by.

When they finally left the caboose, Robert, Amma, and Grandpa Dave thanked the man for showing them the caboose.

"You are very welcome," said the engineer. "Merry Christmas!"

"Merry Christmas to you," they replied.

The three waved goodbye and walked toward the car.

"That was awesome!" Robert's voice vibrated with happiness. "I guess sometimes God does give us the desires of our hearts. I can't wait to tell Mom about our Christmas surprise!"

Melissa's Love Gift

"Look at this X-ray," Dr. Greenlaw told them. "See this narrowing here, and here? And on this 5th vertebra, there is hardly any space or fluid between the vertebra and the spinal cord. You have stenosis of the 5th, 6th, and 7th vertebrae.

"Now, you don't need to stress out about it. Just be careful. You shouldn't lift more than ten pounds. Be careful not to bump your head. And don't get whiplash in a car accident. If you got into a car accident, it wouldn't be good."

Melissa shuddered, and her eyes met Phil's. Concern etched his face.

"I'm sending you to a surgeon for a second opinion," Dr. Greenlaw added. "I don't think you need surgery yet, but we'll see what Dr. McGuire says."

"Okay. Thank you, Dr. Greenlaw." Melissa shook the doctor's hand. She and Phil said goodbye and walked out to the truck.

"Wow, that's scary." Melissa spoke solemnly. "I wonder what could happen if I got into a car accident? Did she mean I would die? Or maybe I would be paralyzed, which might be worse than dying."

They rode in sober silence. When the truck jolted over a rough place in the road, Melissa spoke.

"This truck is so bumpy, and it jars my neck. Do you have heavy-duty springs on it?"

"No, these are just regular springs," Phil replied.

"Is there any way to make it ride more smoothly?" Melissa asked.

"Not that I can think of," answered Phil. "I already have extra weight in the back, with my toolbox. Maybe we should look for a different vehicle."

"Yes, I think we should. If we can find a little car for me that rides more smoothly, you can still have your truck with your tools, and we can use my car on vacations and whenever we go somewhere together. In the meantime, I think I'll get one of those foam-rubber neck braces I've seen some people wearing. Maybe it will stabilize my neck so I won't feel the bumps as much."

> *"You have mild to moderate cervical stenosis," Dr. McGuire told her. "If you are in a car accident or if you fall, you could be paralyzed."*

They drove to Walgreens and Melissa selected a neck brace she thought would fit. On the way home she fastened it around her neck.

"Oh, it's too wide. I thought for sure this would be the right size for my giraffe neck," she chuckled. "That's all right. I'll take the scissors and cut a place for my chin.

"Phil, remember the Toyota Avalon we bought from David and Edie when they moved overseas?" Melissa asked. "They wanted only $600 for it, and it lasted me for more than two years. It rode smoothly, too. I loved that car. I hope we can find one like that."

Over the next few months, they searched the Internet and used-car lots for a small car. The problem was in finding a good car for the amount they could afford.

On November first, Phil drove Melissa to her appointment with the surgeon.

"You have mild to moderate cervical stenosis," Dr. McGuire told her. "If you are in a car accident or if you fall, you could be paralyzed. But surgery could affect your voice box so that you are always hoarse. It could affect your breathing, mess up your jugular veins and carotid arteries, paralyze you, or kill you. The chances of any of these happening are very slim. But if you choose not to get surgery, I certainly wouldn't blame you."

"Oh-h-h-h!" Melissa sputtered. "I certainly choose not to!"

"If you experience numbness often or continually in your hands or fingers, then you should call me. That's when you will need to consider surgery," Dr. McGuire advised.

On the drive home, Melissa felt almost giddy with relief. "I'll be real careful, and probably I won't ever need surgery," she hoped. "I just wish I could find a suitable car for me."

A mile from home, she saw a Chevy Impala for sale. Phil turned around and went back so they could look at it. Melissa did not feel comfortable sitting in it, nor did she like the sound of the engine.

"No, that's not the right one," she told Phil. "It sounds like a piece of junk. Let's keep on looking."

In December, Melissa received a call from her brother Kendall.

"Cyndi bought a new car, and I inherited her old one. We wondered if you could use my Volvo."

"Oh, yes! We have been looking for a car for me! How much do you want for it?"

"Nothing. We will just be happy if it meets your needs."

Tears filled Melissa's eyes as she hung up the phone. Kendall must have heard about her neck problem from a family member. He wanted to give her his car—after the way she had treated him!

Kendall was Melissa's baby brother. When she was five years old, Melissa had fed him and changed him and carried him around on her hip like a little mother. She had loved him with a fierce love, but she lost him when their father left and their family was split up. Baby Kendall had been adopted by a couple in another state. Melissa mourned for him, even while she herself had been sent away twice, and later adopted.

In her late teens, much to her delight, she found Kendall and all of her brothers again. How thrilled she felt when they could spend time together. Kendall had always been special to her. His warm bear hugs and enthusiastic welcomes told her he felt the same way about her. But then something happened, to spoil her joy.

At the lowest point in her life and in deep depression, she had sought the love and companionship of her family, only to overhear Kendall make a negative remark about her. "Well, hasn't she always … ." Try as she might, Melissa could not remember what he had said. She had blocked out the painful memory.

She had been devastated. *So that's what he really thinks of me,* she had thought at the time. It felt like a weight-bearing wall had suddenly been knocked out from under her. From that point on, despite Kendall's hugs she believed that he thought negatively of her.

Years later, it had been Melissa's words that dealt an almost fatal blow to their relationship. She hated confrontation, but she loved Kendall. When she believed he was heading in a direction that could make a mess of his life, she could not in good conscience stand by and let him continue without warning him.

Kendall had taken her concern as an affront. His words and reaction made Melissa even more troubled. She became filled with fear and sadness for him as he went on in his headstrong way. They grew uncomfortable around each other, and the gulf between them widened.

How mean she had been to him during a family-reunion tour of the houses they had lived in as children. The cars had filled up quickly, and only Melissa and Kendall were left to ride in Kendall's car. Disappointed and angry, Melissa had sulked in the front seat, not even carrying on a conversation with Kendall.

The thought had crossed her mind then that perhaps it wasn't a coincidence that they were alone together. Perhaps divine providence had put them together so they could make peace. But Melissa had refused to try. She did not want to be with Kendall, and she was sure he didn't want to be with her. She knew Kendall must have felt her negative thoughts toward him as in silence he drove her on the tour.

And now he was offering to give Melissa his car free of charge. Melissa shook her head in amazement.

Apparently, Kendall is reaching out in love in spite of my meanness on the tour. A few days after the tour I broke out with shingles, and the pain was almost unbearable. I deserved it. I guess I brought it upon myself by my attitude. Oh, forgive me, Lord. Forgive me!

Obviously, Kendall loves me and wants to mend the relationship. He is taking the first step and doing the loving thing by offering me his car. Oh, I wish we could go on a long trip together so we could really get to know each other. All we know is each other's faults. I've never had the opportunity to spend time with him like I have with my other brothers. I believe we would come to enjoy each other in spite of our different personalities and different opinions on some things. I want us to be reconciled.

Just before Christmas, Phil drove Melissa to Greenfield to meet Kendall and Cyndi in the Home Depot parking lot. Kendall showed Melissa the car's features and had her drive him around the parking lot, to familiarize her with the way it handled. Then he handed her an envelope.

"There should be enough in there to get it registered," he said. "Merry Christmas."

Melissa hugged him with awe. She thanked Kendall and Cyndi profusely, but the words fell short of conveying her feelings at that moment. She felt that mere words were entirely inadequate in comparison with the gift of grace she had just been given.

Saying goodbye, she got into the driver's seat and shut the door. Cyndi and Kendall waved as they pulled away in their vehicle. Meekly, carefully, Melissa put the car in gear and followed Phil to the exit. As they turned toward home, her eyes searched the rearview mirror hoping for one last glimpse of Kendall and Cyndi. *Godspeed. Go in peace.*

She approached the traffic circle, tears welling up in her eyes. Kendall had given her his personal car that he loved, that he had driven for years up and down hills, through snow, and sleet, and rain, and dark of night, on missions of mercy. On the tour, she had sat in the passenger seat sullen and angry and rude, and he had, with grace, given up his car for love of her. He could, instead, have sold it for a couple of thousand dollars if he had wanted to. Yet he had given it to her and provided money to get it registered and inspected.

She swiped at both eyes. It would not be good to crash the car on her first time driving it.

She felt his closeness. Kendall had *lived* here. His hands had clutched the steering wheel where her hands now clung. Oh, how she loved him. She knew he had prayed here; no doubt he had sung and laughed and cried here. He had shared journeys and thoughts with Cyndi and with his beloved companion Doberman. And perhaps he had thought of *her* and prayed for *her*.

Maybe Kendall's not perfect. I'm certainly not. But Kendall has shown the true spirit of Christmas—the spirit of Jesus, the spirit of love. With all my heart I hope, and I believe Kendall is hoping as well, that his love gift to me will be a bridge to span the gulf between us in the coming days.

It's been a few years now since Kendall gave Melissa his beloved Volvo. Over time, with the aid of the Holy Spirit, wrong and immature attitudes have been recognized and forsaken. All hurtful words and actions have been forgiven. Kendall's Christmas love gift to Melissa has indeed turned out to be the bridge to a renewed relationship, a relationship they both nurture with peace and good will.

And as of this writing, Melissa has not needed surgery. Her heart is full of gratitude to the heavenly Father, whose Christmas love gift has ever inspired others to give the gift of forgiving love.

Jim's Thawing

Jim shivered in the cold wind and stuffed his hands deeper into his jacket pockets. Christmas lights shone on six inches of new snow, but Jim's warmly-booted feet tramped easily through the plowed streets. A sneer curled his lips.

"Dumb old Dad. He thinks I'm going to Bill's house, but I'm gonna have a good time," he gloated. He felt a twinge of guilt, wondering if his parents would wait up for him as they always did since he had begun hanging around with Kevin and Tony. Jim lit another cigarette. "They're always trying to get me to stop smoking and go back to church," he grumbled. "They don't understand anything."

None of this would have happened if Wendy's parents hadn't taken her away from me, he thought. *What do I have to live for? At least when I'm with my buddies I can forget my heartache for a while. I do feel kind of bad about taking Sis's tithe money, though. Aww, who cares? I'll pay her back later.*

Jim crossed the street and crunched up to Kevin's house. Entering the front door, he left a trail of melting snow up the stairs to the second-floor apartment. At his special rap, the door opened and two faces looked out.

"Tony! You're already here!" exclaimed Jim. "I've got the money. Let's go!"

The three boys trudged down the street to the liquor store, where Tony showed his card and made a purchase. They retraced their steps to the apartment.

A few hours later Kevin hissed, "Sh-h-h!" The rowdy boys froze as a loud knock sounded on the door.

"This is the police! Open up!" The boys stared at each other with anxious eyes. Reluctantly, Kevin opened the door.

"The neighbors are complaining that you boys are making a lot of noise. Don't you know how late it is?" The officer's stern voice matched his frowning face. The boys remained silent. "Do all of you live here?"

Jim and Tony shook their heads.

> *"This is the police! Open up!" The boys stared at each other with anxious eyes.*

"Then you need to get along home. No more noise!"

The policeman left, and Kevin closed the door. In the silence that followed, the boys heard a car door slam, the motor start, and the car drive away.

"Now what do we do?" Kevin asked in a subdued voice. "We can't stay here."

"Let's go to Buddy's Diner! We can get some black coffee and sober up." Jim headed for the door.

"Great idea!" The boys followed him out of the apartment and clomped loudly down the stairs, laughing boisterously.

As they entered the diner, Jim glanced at the clock. "It's midnight. We should have time for a few cups of coffee before the diner closes at one."

At one o'clock, Jim's stupefied brain tried to remember how many cups of coffee he had downed. Four? Five? He could hardly think.

"The coffee didn't help at all," he said. "Maybe by the time I walk home in the cold I'll be sober. See ya." He waved goodbye to his friends.

An idea nagged at his intoxicated mind. *I know; I'll follow the train tracks. They pass close to my house.*

Jim staggered behind the diner to where the tracks were, but he could not detect them under the new snow. Suddenly his boot banged against a rail and he lost his balance and fell headlong across the tracks. Everything went black.

When he came to, he was lying face down in something cold and wet. He lifted his aching head, squinting in the blinding daylight, and looked around. He was lying in a snowbank beside the train tracks. Jim struggled to his knees.

Ouch! I must have banged my knee. Br-r-r, I'm so cold. What happened?

Beside him, extending across the tracks he noticed an indentation about his size, where the snow had partially melted.

I must have fallen onto the tracks. He shook his head, trying to clear the cobwebs. It was hard to think. He looked at the bare rails first in one direction, then in another. A creeping realization made a shudder go through him. *A train must have come through during the night.* An eerie chill inched up his spine. *How did I get off the tracks?*

Jim tried to get his feet under him, but he could not feel them. Snow was packed into the open tops of his sheepskin-lined boots. With a mighty effort, he pushed himself up, swayed for a moment, and then limped slowly away from the tracks toward the street.

Which way was home? His befuddled mind flooded with horror as he realized he did not remember who he was.

How will I find my way home? I don't know who I am, Jim worried. He looked up the street.

There's a telephone booth. Maybe if I read through the names, I'll remember who I am. His numb fingers fumbled with the pages of the telephone book. He squinted at the words, but his blurry eyes could not focus. Disappointed, he resumed his trek up the street, his concern mounting.

At the top of the hill he passed a hospital. Nothing seemed familiar. Jim continued on past the cemetery, around the curve, and down the hill. When he came to Griffin Street, he turned right. At the end of the street, rows of cars lined a parking lot. Jim stared at the sign.

Parker Chevrolet. I recognize that sign. I think I live somewhere near here, he concluded.

By the time Jim got to Morris Street, his memory was coming back. He turned right. Limping down the street, he caught sight of a familiar house.

That's it! That's where I live!

Inside, Jim's mother was crying. By the look of her swollen eyes, she had been crying most of the night.

"Jim! Where have you been," his father shouted. "What kind of a son are you, anyway, making your mother worry all night?"

"I slept in a snowbank," Jim responded. "When I woke up, I didn't know who I was or where I lived, so I began walking, and finally I got here."

"You slept in a snowbank? Take off your boots!" Dad ordered. "Let's see your feet."

Jim tugged and tugged, but his boots were frozen to his feet. His father took a blow dryer and melted first one, and then the other. It seemed to take forever. With great difficulty, his dad at last was able to remove both boots. But Jim's socks would not budge. Again his father used the blow dryer. Finally, he peeled off the socks.

Mother gasped and burst into tears, covering her face with her hands. Jim's feet were black.

"We'd better go to the hospital, Son," Dad said, his anger gone. He helped Jim out to the car and drove him to the hospital.

In the emergency room, Dr. Sandberg sucked in his breath. "Well, those feet are going to have to come off," he said gravely.

"Why start down there, then? You might as well start up here." Jim drew his hand across his throat in a cutting motion. He had no desire to live without feet.

"I want a second opinion," Dad protested.

Miraculously, the other doctor in the hospital that day had treated many soldiers in Korea with frostbitten feet. Dr. Vincent's face looked grim as he examined Jim and his feet and heard his story.

"It's a miracle that you are still alive," Dr. Vincent stated. "You have alcohol poisoning. It's a wonder that you didn't die from it, as many young people do. It's also a wonder that you didn't get hit by a train or freeze to death. You are a very lucky young man."

"As for your feet … ." Dr. Vincent stroked his beard, thoughtful.

"I think we can save them," he said at last. "But it isn't going to be easy—especially for you."

Dr. Vincent ordered blood thinners and other medications and admitted Jim to the hospital. Over the next six weeks, Jim experienced indescribable pain, the worst pain he had ever felt. At first his feet felt like they were on fire, while the rest of his body shivered violently in the 80-degree warmth of the hospital. Because of the pain, Jim could not bear to have a blanket or even a sheet covering his feet. As the circulation slowly began to return, he experienced a terrible tingling in addition to the burning. The torture seemed to go on for an eternity.

After Dr. Vincent had done all he could, Jim's feet had only 40 percent circulation and the nerves were dead. He would no longer be able to feel if his feet were freezing, so he would need to be extremely careful in the cold.

As if he had not suffered enough, upon Jim's discharge he was summoned before a judge. The police had suspected Jim of trying to kill himself on the tracks. The judge ordered a month of counseling in a psychiatric hospital. To Jim, the experience seemed like a nightmare. Ultimately, however, good came from it. The staff were kind to him, and with their encouragement he began learning to walk again. Because Jim had been in bed and in a wheelchair for so long, his legs and feet were very weak. But eventually, about six months after his feet froze, Jim was able to walk normally in spite of the damaged nerves.

Christmas came once again. Jim spent the holiday at home with his parents and his sister, who had forgiven him. As they reviewed the experiences of the past year, strong emotions flooded over Jim—relief that it was all over, gratefulness that he had not died there in the snow or on the tracks, thankfulness that he still had feet to walk on, and amazement at God's faithfulness even when *he* hadn't been faithful.

"I'll never get drunk again," Jim vowed. And he didn't.

In fact, as the years passed, Jim allowed God to change him completely. Looking back, Jim and his family can see that the thawing of Jim's feet began the thawing of Jim's heart.

The Christmas That Almost Was

"Will this rain ever stop?" Brian's voice sounded as dismal as the weather. Brian and I and our eight-year-old daughter, Geri, had moved to Enumclaw, Washington, totally unprepared for the climate. Sometimes it rained, other times it poured, often it drizzled, and now and then the dark, cloudy skies simply pouted. Through a shower we drove to Geri's school. Through a cloudburst we drove to our low-paying temporary jobs. In the foggy mist we drove home again. The sun peeked out occasionally just to taunt us and let us know it was still there. The three of us felt gloomier than Eeyore the donkey standing in a mud hole during a heavy downpour, having lost his tail.

We were living in a small travel trailer at the little country airport until we could get back on our feet financially. Our wet shoes tracked mud all over the carpet. The towels never dried completely, and even the bed sheets felt damp and cold. Miserably homesick for New England and for the family members we had left behind, we were about as low as we could go. It had felt good to move away and start over, but now I wondered if we had made the right decision. I missed my teenage daughter, Angie, terribly and regretted leaving her behind.

The upcoming Christmas parade promised a bright moment in our otherwise dreary lives. But, of course, when the day for the parade came, it was raining—a heavy mist that only made us more miserable. I squeezed under the rear edge of a stranger's large umbrella, shivering. It seemed so weird to see Santa Claus behind his eight reindeer, waving to us through the rain. Why couldn't it have snowed, if it couldn't be sunny?

The country music that played all day long at my workplace only contributed to my melancholy. Most of the songs seemed to be about alcohol, bars, or failed relationships. I appreciated the songs about commitment and happiness, and tried to tune out the others. Incredibly, in spite of the frequent rain, Eddie Rabbit's "I Love a Rainy Night" became a favorite, although I waited in vain to wake up to the sunny day the lyrics promised.

That first week of December, as I concentrated on my work and turned a deaf ear to the radio, the phrase *one thousand dollars* caught my attention. I stopped working and listened. The deejay explained that the radio station would give away a thousand dollars each day to the first caller who could give the names of three announced songs and their vocal artists. The station would choose three of the songs played during the day, so I needed to pay attention and write down the names. The call-in would take place every evening. I became excited. With a thousand dollars, Angie could fly out for Christmas!

From then on, I kept one ear on the radio as I did my work. When I described the thousand-dollar-a day giveaway to Geri and Brian, Geri's clouded eyes lit up.

"You know, the chance of your winning is infinitesimally small," Brian cautioned, not wanting me to get my hopes up. He liked big words. I couldn't even pronounce it.

"I know," I agreed. "But maybe God will work a miracle. Maybe He will do something really special for us this Christmas."

Brian gave me a look that said he didn't think so. Brian doubted that there was a God.

Some days I missed a song while I ate lunch or concentrated on my work. Each day that I heard the three chosen songs, I phoned the radio station in the evening as soon as the deejay announced the call-in. And every time, I heard a busy signal. I hung up and dialed again and again until I heard the deejay speak to the winning caller on the radio.

Two weeks before Christmas, I again dialed the radio station's number, expecting to hear the busy signal. The sound of ringing startled me.

"It's ringing," I shouted. Brian's and Geri's faces broke into smiles, anticipating the happy Christmas we were about to have. The radio deejay's voice droned on and on as the phone rang again and again in my ear.

An urgent feeling came. *Turn off the radio.* I had been told there was a delay between the radio and the phone that might confuse a person.

But Brian and Geri were listening to the radio. Should I tell them to turn it off? As I hesitated, the phone continued ringing and the announcer's voice continued to blare from the radio. The feeling came again, *Turn off the radio.*

Assuming that the radio station had two or three phone lines, I figured the deejay's office assistant would answer the first line right away and say, "Please hold." Then when the deejay was ready, he would press a button to speak to the caller. As the phone rang relentlessly, I began to suspect that the assistant had answered the first caller and had left my line ringing.

"They're not answering," I said. "They probably already picked up a line."

> *The varied noises were stressful and confusing. But I hung on, desperately hoping that maybe, just maybe, God would do something to lift us from depression and homesickness.*

"Hold on! Don't hang up!" Brian and Geri hollered.

The varied noises were stressful and confusing. But I hung on, desperately hoping that maybe, just maybe, God would do something to lift us from depression and homesickness. Maybe I would be the caller to win a thousand dollars!

Quickly I reviewed the names of the three songs and their artists. Just then the phone clicked and I heard the deejay's voice.

"This is radio station KCRB. You are our first caller. Do you have the names of today's songs and their vocal artists?"

"Yes! "Keeper of the Stars" by Tracy Byrd, "Forever and Ever, Amen" by Randy Travis, and "I Love a Rainy Night" by Eddie Rabbit.

"Congratulations! You just won a thousand dollars," the deejay said.

"Thank God! Thank God!" I sobbed, overcome with emotion and relief. Angie could come for Christmas! A ray of hope shone through the clouds of gloom.

"What is your first name?" the deejay asked kindly.

"Brie," I blubbered.

"Well, Brie, what will you do with a thousand dollars?" the deejay questioned.

"I'll buy a plane ticket for my daughter to come for Christmas! We've been so lonesome for her. Thank you *very much*! God bless you for doing this."

The deejay wished us a Merry Christmas and transferred the line to his assistant. I gave her my name and address and hung up the phone. Brian turned off the radio.

"We won!" I bawled. Brian and Geri yelled and hugged each other.

By another miracle we were able to get Angie on a plane on Christmas Day! We hardly noticed the rain as we drove to the Seattle airport. How beautiful Angie was, with a huge smile on her face, running to throw her arms around us. I ran, too, with tears streaming down my face. It was, indeed, the happiest Christmas ever. It was one more powerful evidence to Brian that God lives and cares for us, and his disbelief at that point began to change to gratefulness and faith.

Wiping tears from my eyes, I came back to reality. That is what *should* have happened. I have played the scenes over and over in my mind ever since that fateful night when I stood in our tiny trailer kitchen, listening to the ringtone of the radio station phone. This is what actually happened:

"They're not answering," I said. "They probably already picked up a line."

"Hold on! Don't hang up!" Brian and Geri hollered.

"But they're not answering. Why did I think things would get better, anyway?" I grumbled dejectedly.

"Don't hang up! Don't hang up!" Geri and Brian pleaded.

"I probably dialed the wrong number. That figures," I growled.

The many sounds were so confusing. Br-r-r-r-t! *Turn off the radio*. Br-r-r-r-t! "Don't hang up! Don't hang up!" Br-r-r-r-t-! "And so far, we have given away $10,000." Br-r-r-r-t! B-r-r-r-t! In the middle of all that nerve-racking noise, I let the depression and hopelessness I had been feeling for weeks take over. I lost faith that God would do something good for us in our dark hours. I hung up.

Just then the deejay said, "And now we are ready to pick today's winner!" He pushed the phone button. Over the radio speaker came a long, flat dial tone.

"I hate to tell you, but you just hung up on a thousand dollars," the deejay said. Brian switched off the radio.

"Mom, you hung up on a thousand dollars," Geri protested. "Why did you give up? Why didn't you keep hanging on?"

"That wasn't me," I snapped. "He wasn't talking about me. That was a different caller." Brian's face looked sad as he turned away.

Christmas came and went, with the same rain, the same gloom, the same hopelessness. We wallowed in our misery and somehow got through it. My family kindly never brought up the subject or blamed me for our dismal Christmas. Angie spent an uneventful Christmas in New England with her father and stepmother. Eventually the rain stopped and we enjoyed a whole month of sunny days—in August.

> I had let my feelings keep God from giving us the fantastic Christmas present He wanted to give. Collapsing under pressure, I had chosen despair, depression, and hopelessness instead of faith.

It probably took until August before I could admit my mistake, even to myself. It was just too horrible to believe. I had let my feelings keep God from giving us the fantastic Christmas present He wanted to give. Collapsing under pressure, I had chosen despair, depression, and hopelessness instead of faith. Not only had I disappointed my family, but I also had caused Angie to miss out on the wonderful Christmas she could have spent with us. Even worse, I had kept Brian from seeing one more powerful evidence of God's existence, love, and care. Now I wondered if he would *ever* believe. Only time would tell.

I was sure of one thing, though. No longer would I let depression and despondency dictate my decisions. Instead, I would choose to trust, to keep hanging on, no matter what. I would choose to be cheerful and sweet and to encourage those around me.

Although I regret the Christmas that almost was, I look forward with hope to other Christmases—and especially to the eternal Christmas in heaven where Angie will be with us forever and ever.

Amen.

Little Kitty

Little Kitty was a white and gray kitten. Her eyes were yellow.

Little Kitty was a happy little kitten. But today she was sad. She was lost and afraid. She was cold.

Little Kitty hid in the bushes. At night she came out to look for food.

Little Kitty found a bowl of food. Big Yellow Cat hissed at her. Little Kitty hissed and growled. Her fur stood up, making her look bigger.

Yellow Cat backed away. His tail swished angrily. Little Kitty ate and ate and ate. Her tummy felt good.

Little Kitty found a warm bed. Big Yellow Cat hissed at her. Little Kitty hissed and growled. Her fur stood up, making her look bigger.

Yellow Cat backed away. His tail swished angrily. Little Kitty curled up in the warm bed. She slept and slept.

In the morning, Yellow Cat took a walk with his family. Little Kitty went, too. She rubbed her head on Yellow Cat. Yellow Cat hissed at her.

Little Kitty found a mouse. She played and played. Yellow Cat sat down and watched.

Yellow Cat's family petted Little Kitty's back. Little Kitty felt afraid. She tried to scratch.

Then she purred and rubbed her head on the people's hands.

"Little Kitty," the people said. "We like you very much. But Big Yellow Cat lives here. You cannot live here. We must find you a home."

They put Little Kitty into a box. She could not feel the cold wind anymore. Little Kitty was finally warm. She lay down in the sun in the box and purred.

The people took Little Kitty down the road. Little Kitty saw a barn.

"Here is a good home for you, Little Kitty." Little Kitty went inside.

A donkey hee-hawed hello. A cow mooed softly. Mice played in the straw.

Little Kitty saw a baby in the manger. The baby's parents smiled at Little Kitty.

Little Kitty jumped up. She pushed her paws up and down, up and down, in the warm hay. She purred a happy song. Then she lay down by the baby's feet.

Little Kitty purred and purred. She was home at last.

Sacrifice of Love

"Goldie, would you like to go visit Paulie?" Mother asked.

"Yes!" Five-year-old Goldie jumped up and down for joy. She and her seven-year-old brother, Paul, were best buddies. Paul had been staying at the Sullivans' farm for a few months, and she had been as forlorn as a little lost lamb without him.

"I'll visit him for two weeks," Goldie decided. "Then I'll be back."

"Come, then, and let's give you a bath. Nona's mom says you can have a bath in her big sink, with bubbles."

Goldie hugged herself with excitement and danced down the stairs. She loved nooks and crannies and unusual places, and had always thought what great fun it would be to take a bath in their neighbor's deep kitchen sink. And Mother was promising bubbles as well! Hunkering down under a thick layer of bubbles, Goldie sang a happy little song as Mother washed her arms and chest.

"I'm going to see Paulie, see Paulie, see Paulie; I'm going to see Paulie today. I'm going to pet kitties and see baby cowsies; I'm going to see Paulie today."

Mother was quiet. Her hands moved slowly. Goldie looked up into her mother's face. Were those tears in Mother's eyes? Why would Mother be sad? Goldie was going on a big adventure, to see Paulie! No, she must have imagined the tears.

Dressed in warm clothes and her hand-me-down wool plaid peacoat, Goldie ran out the door to where Dolly was waiting with the little red wagon. Hopping in, Goldie settled herself. Mother came out of the house carrying a large brown paper bag.

"Here are your clothes," she said.

"Oh, thank you!" smiled Goldie, holding the bag on her lap. "I almost forgot!"

Mother bent her head close to Goldie.

"Mother has to kiss you goodbye," she said. She gave Goldie a lin-gering kiss, then turned away and walked rapidly toward the house.

> *Goldie looked up into her mother's face. Were those tears in Mother's eyes?*

Goldie felt a twinge of sadness. She would miss Mother. But she was going to see Paulie! Anticipation thrilled her as Dolly pulled her down the street to where they would meet the pastor who would take her to see Paulie.

At first, Goldie looked out the car window and watched the grass and trees flash by. The hum of the car tires made her sleepy. Finally, she couldn't keep her eyes open anymore.

Goldie awoke in an unfamiliar bed in an unfamiliar room. A boy in pajamas was staring down at her. Fear coursed through her.

A lady entered the room. "Good morning! I am Mrs. Swanson, the pastor's wife. This is our son, Wayne. Wayne, please go and get dressed."

Wayne left the room. Mrs. Swanson smiled at Goldie. "Let's get you washed and dressed. After you eat breakfast, I'll drive you to where Mrs. Sullivan works, and she will take you to the farm to see your brother."

Soon the pastor's wife left Goldie with Mrs. Sullivan. Before they went to the farm, Mrs. Sullivan bought Goldie a pretty blue coat. Goldie felt terrified of all the strangers. She clung to Mrs. Sullivan's skirt as they traipsed in and out of stores. Finally, they drove to the farm, and Goldie met Mr. Sullivan. He seemed pleasant, but the scar on his face frightened her. Goldie decided to be cautious until she knew he could be trusted.

After a very long wait, a school bus screeched to a stop in front of the farm, and Paulie ran down the steps with a surprised look on his face. Goldie ran to him and threw her arms around his neck. At last she was with her beloved Paulie.

What fun they had together! Goldie laughed out loud as Paulie ran up and down the bumpy dirt driveway, pulling her in his new red wagon. Sometimes he slid open the barn door and they entered its cool, dark recesses that smelled of hay. As they climbed the wall ladder to the hayloft, startled pigeons fled out the barn window. Barn swallows flew in and out and fed their babies in mud nests overhead. They played hide-and-seek among the hay bales and Goldie squealed with delight when she discovered a nest of newborn kittens. At milking time, they watched the hired man milk the cows by hand, squirting milk first into a bucket and then into the mouth of a waiting cat. Goldie loved to pet the black-and-white Holstein cows and the red-and-white Guernseys, but Pixie, the cream-colored Jersey, soon became her favorite.

Occasionally Paulie pushed one of the antique open buggies out into the dooryard. He drove it by running along between the huge front and back wooden spoke wheels while pushing and steering the front wheel. Goldie sat like a lady upon the cushioned seat, pretending she was a princess drawn by beautiful horses.

After a couple of weeks, Goldie wondered when she would be going home. No one had mentioned it, not even the pastor at church. She and Paulie discussed the subject in uneasy whispers. Finally, Goldie summoned her courage.

"When will the pastor take me home?" she asked Mr. and Mrs. Sullivan.

"Oh, don't you want to stay a while longer and play with Paulie?" they coaxed. Goldie shook her head. She was homesick.

One night after Goldie had been put to bed upstairs in the farmhouse, silent tears slid down the sides of her face and into her ears. When would the Sullivans let her go home? She hungered for her family. Suddenly, an icy hand of fear clutched her heart, and she *knew*. They were never going to let her go home! Mother had not sent her to play with Paulie for a while, she had given her away! Goldie buried her face in her pillow and wailed over and over again, "I want my mommy! I want my fam'ly!"

As the weeks passed, farm life with Paulie was the most fun Goldie had ever had. Mr. and Mrs. Sullivan were very nice, too. One day, Mrs. Sullivan asked Goldie and Paulie to call them Mother and Father.

Violently, Goldie clenched her teeth. *"I already have a mother and a father!"* But her tender heart could not bear to hurt the Sullivans for long. After a few days she obeyed their wishes, hoping her mother and father would forgive her.

Although they missed their family, Paul and Goldie grew to love their new parents, and thrived among the cows and kittens in the pastoral beauty of Vermont. Spring and summer faded into fall, and school began.

As Christmas approached, Goldie exchanged eager whispers with Paulie about what Santa Claus would bring them. She longed for a walking doll, while Paulie wished for an Erector Set®, a construction kit consisting of a variety of many-holed metal strips with real screws and nuts, pulleys, and a small motor. One could build lots of amazing structures with an Erector Set!

A few weeks before Christmas, some friends brought them an early Christmas gift, an Uncle Wiggily board game. Goldie adored rabbits and immediately fell in love with Uncle Wiggily's picture on the box lid. He reminded her of the brown bunny they had owned at their original home. Goldie could hardly wait to play the game.

"Mother, come and play Uncle Wiggily with us!" she begged as soon as their friends had gone.

Mother opened the box and read the directions, and soon cardboard figures of Uncle Wiggily were being hopped around the game board. Uncle Wiggily was so much fun to play! Never had Goldie enjoyed a gift or a toy as much as she enjoyed Uncle Wiggily.

Just before Christmas, Aunt Agnes came by with news about a family whose house had burned down. All of their toys had been destroyed in the fire. Paulie and Goldie sat motionless in the playroom among their toys as Mother and Aunt Agnes discussed the misfortune in the living room.

Presently Mother called, "Paul, Goldie!" They left the playroom and went to her.

"Would you like to give some Christmas presents to the little girl and boy whose house burned?"

"Yes!" they cried simultaneously.

"Why don't you go through your toys and choose some to give them?" Mother suggested. "We'll wrap them, and Aunt Agnes will take them over to where the family is staying."

Goldie glanced at Paulie, then headed to the playroom to see which toys she could spare. It was exciting to think of giving the children gifts, but oh, it was hard to part with her loved toys. She couldn't do without her Farmall® tractor! Anyway, the paint was almost worn off.

Eventually Goldie selected a few decent-looking toys that she really didn't care about and placed them with Paulie's. Gazing thoughtfully at the small pile of toys, she felt a little ashamed. Somewhere in the past she had learned that God loves a cheerful giver, one who gives from the heart.

Give your best, a voice inside her seemed to say.

My best? Why, that would be Uncle Wiggily. But I don't *want* to give him; I *love* rabbits.

Do unto others as you would have them do unto you, whispered the inner voice. *Give your best*. Goldie imagined the little girl opening a present on Christmas morning and finding Uncle Wiggily. She knew the little girl would be very happy to have such a fun game to play.

And maybe she likes rabbits, too, the voice reasoned.

But it would hurt to give him away. My heart would ache. Uncle Wiggily is my favorite thing in the whole world.

Be unselfish; give from a heart of love, the voice urged.

But I love Uncle Wiggily.

Back and forth, back and forth, Goldie wrestled with herself. First she felt a wistful longing for Uncle Wiggily, and intense emotional pain at the thought of giving him up. Then she thought of the little girl's pleasure. Could she make the sacrifice? She could hear the clock ticking away the minutes as she hesitated.

Finally, Goldie reached for Uncle Wiggily. "Paul, do you want to give them Uncle Wiggily?" she asked.

"But it's new. We've only played it once."

"I know. But wouldn't it be nice for them to have a new game instead of only used toys?"

"Well, okay. Go ahead."

Goldie felt her heart was tearing in two as she placed Uncle Wiggily on top of the pile of toys. But she did not change her mind.

"Mother, we're done," she called.

Mother brought a box. She hesitated when she saw Uncle Wiggily. "Are you sure you want to give away your new game?" she asked doubtfully.

"Yes. Jesus wants us to give our best. I love Uncle Wiggily, and I want the little girl who lost her home to have him."

Mother turned back to the toys and began gathering them up. Her eyes must have been itching, because she rubbed them.

Goldie is grown up now. Looking back, she feels that was one of the most difficult and painful decisions of her childhood. For years she yearned for Uncle Wiggily. Yet, of the childhood Christmases she remembers, that was the happiest Christmas of all. Yes, she received a walking doll, and Paul got his Erector Set. But what made it the happiest was imagining a little girl's surprise and delight on Christmas morning as she tore open the Christmas paper and found Uncle Wiggily. Thinking of the little girl's happiness brought a warming joy to Goldie's heart—the deep, quiet joy that comes from a sacrifice of love.

Years later, Goldie learned that her birth mother also had made a sacrifice of love. Their father was no longer there, and Mother was sick and couldn't provide for her children. Their mother struggled back and forth, praying and crying, wanting to keep her beloved children but wanting them to have enough food and clothes. Finally, she did the unselfish thing—she did what was best for her children in spite of her breaking heart. Like our heavenly Father who gave His Son for us, she made a loving sacrifice for the good of others. In doing so, she brought joy to the Sullivans, who had no children. When making her decision, she was unaware that Goldie and Paul were suffering from malnutrition and tuberculosis. Under Mrs. Sullivan's skilled nursing care, with fresh garden produce and clear country air, Goldie and Paulie overcame both malnutrition and tuberculosis.

With a forgiving heart, Goldie gratefully acknowledges that if it were not for her mother's loving sacrifice, she and Paulie likely would have died. And Goldie knows that surely there must be a God in heaven who loves her and who causes all things to work together for good to those who love Him (see Rom. 8:28).

Christmas Comes to Emily

Emily carefully picked her way around an icy patch on the sidewalk. *Why doesn't Christmas feel happy?* she wondered. *I have been really looking forward to this walk with my husband to the Christmas Eve service, but it seems empty.* Reaching a clear place, she looked up at the stars. They twinkled from between the bare branches of the maples and sat like Christmas lights on the tips of silhouetted evergreens.

"Look at the beautiful stars," she exclaimed at the sight that usually filled her with happiness. Tonight her words fell flat. The stars did nothing to brighten her mood. Even a glimpse of her favorite constellation, Orion, did not cheer her.

That was the way she felt—like she was peering through a mist trying to get in touch with her feelings.

This rare opportunity to spend Christmas alone with Ryan seems joyless, she mused. *What is wrong with me? I should be thrilled at this treasure of time together. Am I depressed? Even setting up the nativity felt boring. I don't know. It just doesn't feel like Christmas.*

As they crossed the bridge, Emily lingered to peer over the railing. Her eyes could not penetrate the white mist hiding the dark river from view. That was the way she felt—like she was peering through a mist trying to get in touch with her feelings.

They entered the warm church and found a seat. Emily gazed with affection on the church she had been custodian of when her daughter was a baby. How lovely the crèche looked with softly flickering candles around it. But where were the red poinsettias that usually graced the railing above? Oh! There was the section of balcony where Alexis, in her walker, had tumbled down two steps and crashed into the railing, jabbing her new tooth through her lip. Emily shuddered. Her eyes explored the ceiling and discovered large chips of paint curling from the designs. A feeling of sadness overwhelmed her. The church had aged. *So have I,* she thought wearily.

A baby grand piano almost blocked the door to the right of the pulpit. With alarm, Emily noticed a young man tuning his violin and a young girl steadying her cello. Were they not going to use the pipe organ? How she had loved its robust tones! In the shadow of the balcony stood a small choir with sheet music, listening as the music director gave them last-minute instructions. Irritation rose inside her. None of these had been there when Alexis was a baby. *Why do people have to change things? Just give me the service plain and simple like it was years ago.* With a heavy sigh, she tried to arrange herself more comfortably on the straight-backed pew. The piano, cello, and violin began the prelude. In spite of her irritation, the music seemed to soothe her.

As the service began, a shot of joy ran through her veins. They were using the pipe organ, after all! Singing the beloved carols and listening to the scriptures of Jesus' birth, she felt the tension begin to leave her. The service had remained essentially the same. And the occasional pieces by the new musicians were incredibly beautiful. They added a nice touch, she had to admit.

Somewhere in the middle of the hour, Emily realized the cold, numb feeling inside her had dispersed. The peace that was all around her—in the quiet, candlelit church, in the carols and readings, in the faces of the worshippers—softly stole into her heart.

Why, this is the essence of Christmas—reverently worshipping the Lord Jesus with those who love Him, too. No wonder I have felt so detached from Christmas. In the holiday rush, I took no time to be quiet, to reflect on the meaning of God's amazing gift to me, and to thank Him. No wonder I was weary and irritable; no wonder it didn't feel like Christmas.

With a grateful heart, Emily lit her candle and smiled up into Ryan's shining face, feeling at one with the candlelit faces singing "Silent Night" around her in the darkened church. Following the prayer, with bated breath she listened to the bell in the clock tower peal the joyful tones of midnight. *Christ is born!* He was born anew in her heart.

They warmed themselves at one of the wood stoves before going out into the night. At the bridge the mist had dissipated, and Emily could see the peaceful river flowing between its frozen edges. Were the stars shining more brilliantly now through the bare branches? Orion seemed to be smiling from his new position in the sky. She and Ryan chatted happily as they stepped together over the icy places, her arm tightly anchored in his. She thought that it just might be a perfect night, after all.

But heaven was about to put the finishing touch on Emily's Christmas Eve. On a large, unavoidable stretch of ice, without warning, both of Ryan's feet slid out in front of him and he fell backward. Miraculously, Emily's feet, planted on the same ice, did not slip. To her amazement, her arm held firm as a rock while Ryan got his feet under him and pulled himself upright again.

As they continued their journey home, awe crept over her. There was no way her arm could have remained unmovable and lifted Ryan's body. Someone must have helped her. Surely the angels that sang at Jesus' birth had come to her.

She smiled in quiet joy as warmth, like a hug, spread over her. She was loved!

Christmas, indeed, had come to Emily.

With a Grandmother's Heart

That was my cell phone. I fumbled for it, pressed the button, and held it to my ear.

"Hello?"

"Katie, Marie had the baby. It's a little girl, and she's not doing well. She's in the neonatal intensive care unit at UMass. Marie is okay, but we're all worried about the baby. Her chances aren't good, at only seven months."

"Oh, no. Thank you for letting me know. Tell Marie I'll be there as soon as I can."

Tears flooded my eyes, and love flooded my heart for a baby granddaughter I didn't even know. My first grandchild.

"Please, God! Take care of that little baby. I want her to live! Give Marie strength."

A few hours later, I stood by the incubator, gently holding the tiny hand of my precious granddaughter. Tubes and wires were attached to her tiny body that was clothed only with a diaper. I hoped she was warm. I willed her to live. I sent all the love I had to her little body, hoping she could feel it. When I had to leave the NICU, I stood outside the door, praying, longing for God to make her well. How I wished I could hold her in my arms and comfort her.

All the love in my grandmother's heart and in Marie's heart was not enough to help Danielle overcome her health issues. She passed away in her mother's arms, leaving a giant hole in her mother's heart, and one in mine.

Life went on somehow. Eventually we were able to laugh again. Perhaps one day we will be able to think of her without tears. Although we can no longer hold Danielle in our arms, we will hold her forever in our hearts.

Brighter days came. Christmas was in the air. Marie planned a special outing for her sister, Laurieanne, and me. She and her boyfriend took us to the IMAX® Theater at Justin's Furniture.

We toured the showrooms, exclaiming over the furniture displays that were decorated for Christmas, and eventually ended up in the theater. The young folks buckled themselves into movable seats, but I declined their invitation and sat down instead where a few benches had been placed for the faint of heart.

Soon the action movie began. Watching it, I was very glad I wasn't in one of those movable seats. The audience felt as though they were in a fast-moving car, and screamed every time it seemed they were going to crash.

Not far into the movie, a nearby movement grabbed my attention. One of the attendants was unbuckling a little boy about four years old who looked terrified and was having an emotional meltdown. The attendant lifted him down from the seat and placed him on the bench in front of me, then walked away.

The movie was almost deafening. The boy's shoulders jerked spasmodically, and I could tell he was crying. Quickly I searched the audience to see if his mother was concerned. It seemed that no one had missed him. Everyone was fully involved in the movie.

I couldn't leave him there, scared to death, crying and alone. After all, I was a grandmother! Or at least I *had* been, for one week. Leaning forward, I touched his shoulder gently and spoke into his ear.

"Do you want to sit on my lap?"

He nodded and climbed over the bench. I lifted him onto my lap and wrapped my arms around him.

"The movie is loud and the seats move and make you feel like you're in the car. It's very scary, but the movie won't hurt us. I'll stay right here with you."

"My little girl once was very frightened by a movie, and she got on my lap, too. She was about your age."

I cannot describe the happiness and the bittersweet of those moments, as I sat cuddling a little one just as I had cuddled my own daughters and would never be able to cuddle my granddaughter.

We sat through the rest of the movie together, my heart warmed with love and sympathy for a frightened little boy.

When the movie ended, he stayed on my lap, in no hurry to leave. The people stepped down from their seats. I spotted a lady about ten feet in front of us, searching. Spying the boy on my lap, she frowned angrily.

"Morgan, shame on you! Get down!" she scolded. I thought she would come over to get him and find out what had happened, but she didn't.

Obediently, Morgan climbed down from my lap.

"Thank you for sitting with me and helping me not to be scared," I told him.

He went to his mom. Angrily she grabbed his hand and glared back at me accusingly, as though I were an evil person.

I knew I should go and introduce myself and tell her why I was holding him on my lap. But I was an abuse survivor, and the fear of her anger was stronger than my desire to set her mind at ease. I hoped Morgan would tell her, but I think it remained just a warm memory in both of our hearts.

We sat through the rest of the movie together, my heart warmed with love and sympathy for a frightened little boy.

Morgan's mother, I don't blame you for your reaction. I once responded in anger out of fear when I thought I had lost my daughter and found her with strangers. I hope you will realize that I had no evil intentions. With a grandmother's heart, I filled in for you when you were not available, just as I would have wanted you to do for my little granddaughter in a similar situation. I felt it an honor to be able to comfort your son when you couldn't. Perhaps it was God who put me there at just the right time, because He loves your son and was watching over him.

The years have flown by. I have two grandsons and two granddaughters, all dearly loved, some of them old enough now to have babes of their own. I am truly blessed.

And forever in my heart I hold a tiny baby girl. And a warm, happy memory of a sweet little boy.

When the Radio Station Went Silent

Lori closed her genetics textbook with a bang and took out her notes to review before it was time to meet with her speech professor. Her speech would be the culmination of everything she had learned in class, and the sole grade for the class. On top of that, she was studying for finals in all of her other subjects. She was a diligent student, but it was difficult for her 40-something brain to master the concepts of college genetics, having had no background in genetics in high school. They weren't yet teaching genetics when she was in high school! And chemistry had never been her favorite subject. It remained equally boring and confusing even now.

Why am I doing this? she asked herself. *I feel overwhelmed. I'm so exhausted and I don't know how I can possibly study all this stuff in time for exams. And be a mother of a 16-year-old daughter and shop and cook and pay the bills? I wish I was done with this speech. It's taking up time that I need for studying.*

She checked her wristwatch, packed her notes into her backpack, and maneuvered the bike out the front door.

The bike was really too tall for her short legs. They had found the bike with a broken axle abandoned in the vacant lot next to their house, while searching for a mewing kitten. They had informed the police and waited the appropriate time for someone to claim the bike. Now it was theirs, along with the happy kitten. The bike was just the right size for Katelyn's long legs, so she had claimed it. She attended a grade school too far away to ride and gladly let her mother use the bike for the mile to the college in order to save gasoline.

As Lori rode, she thought of an incident that had taken place two weeks earlier.

Having gotten a late start on that day, she was standing on the bike pedals, pumping as fast as her legs could go. Since the campus was nearly empty, she raced across on the sidewalk, guiding the bike to the edge to pass safely a young man coming toward her. She misjudged and her front tire slipped off the sidewalk and into a groove between the sidewalk and the grass. The bike stopped and fell sideways. Instinctively, she went limp and rolled with the fall, finally coming to a stop on her back with her knees up. She opened her eyes. The young man she had tried to avoid stood peering down at her anxiously.

"Are you all right?" he asked with concern in his voice.

Thinking of how funny a woman with gray hair at her temples must have looked falling off a bike and rolling over and over, Lori burst into peals of laughter.

Thinking of how funny a woman with gray hair at her temples must have looked falling off a bike and rolling over and over, Lori burst into peals of laughter.

"Yes, I'm all right," she assured him. He lingered, wondering, so she jumped up and went over and picked up the bike. Her laughter rang out across the campus toward the young man's retreating back.

Lori laughed again at the memory.

"At least I'm not running late this time," she told herself. Her teacher, Dr. Taylor, required her to give the speech for him as practice before she gave it in class the following day. She parked the bike in a rack and ran up the stairs to the classroom. Dr. Taylor was waiting for her.

"Hello, Dr. Taylor. I hope you haven't been waiting long."

"You're on time. Go ahead and begin when you are ready."

"Since I am planning to become a doctor, I chose a medical subject. The title of my talk is 'Osteoporosis.'"

Lori began her speech. As it continued, she became distressed and agitated. She could not remember her notes and had to keep reading her 3″ x 5″ cards. In addition, it was evident that her talk was dull and lifeless.

"This is awful! I feel terrible that you have to sit and listen to it."

"Continue," directed Dr. Taylor.

After a few more minutes, Lori was so disgusted that she felt she couldn't proceed. But Dr. Taylor insisted on hearing all of her speech.

Lori floundered through to the end and left the campus discouraged. She knew her grade would not be higher than a D, if that.

"I have to fix this," she spoke to herself. "Even if it takes all night. My other studies will have to wait."

She picked Katelyn up from school and made supper. Katelyn did her homework and went to bed. Lori sat at the table, rearranging her talk.

"I know! I'll begin with the story of my falling off my bike! That should get their attention. It fits right in with my subject." Far into the night she rewrote and rearranged her note cards. It was 3:00 a.m. before she felt satisfied at last and went to bed.

The next morning Lori nervously rode the bike to the college and parked it. Walking to class, she felt terrified of giving her speech in front of her much younger classmates and her teacher.

I hope my turn is first so I can get it over with, she said to herself. But she was next to last. She gathered her notes and stepped to the front of the room.

"A couple of weeks ago, I was riding my bike across campus ... ." When Lori got to the part where the young man stood peering down at her, the room erupted in laughter. So far, so good. But now Lori had to make the transition to her subject. She began to tremble. The room became as quiet as the snowflakes drifting down outside the window.

"If I had had osteoporosis, that fall probably would have resulted in at least one broken bone."

She made it through the talk, and gaining confidence, she sailed through the question-and-answer period, even causing laughter again by one of her creative answers. And then it was over. She had done it! And it was good. Probably she would get at least a C. It would lower her GPA, but not as much as a D or an F would have.

After Katelyn had gone to bed, Lori poured herself a drink of water and tuned the radio to the Christian station, hoping to hear Christmas carols. She opened her genetics book and soon became engrossed in her studies.

During one particularly difficult section of study, Lori suddenly realized the room had gone silent. She vaguely remembered having heard an instrumental rendition of "Silent Night." Now the silence caught her attention.

With alarm, she thought, "Oh no! Something happened to the radio station output and the sound isn't coming through."

After waiting another minute, she hurriedly searched for the phone number and dialed the station. The phone rang a couple of times before a man answered.

"Radio Station KFLQ."

"Something happened to your output! There is no sound!" Lori practically shouted.

"I'm sorry, what?" the man asked, sounding confused.

"Something must have happened to the sound because it's not coming over my radio. It was playing 'Silent Night' and suddenly everything went silent."

"Thank you for calling and letting me know," said the deejay.

"You're welcome," responded Lori.

She returned to her genetics book, feeling proud that she had done a good deed. The deejay would find the problem, quickly remedy it, and soon the airwaves would be humming again, bringing happiness to thousands of satisfied customers.

About ten minutes passed, and the room remained quiet. Lori wondered why the station operator had not been able to fix the problem. She felt sympathy for his embarrassment and for all the listeners who had lost their programming.

But then she remembered. When the station operator had answered the phone, she had heard the radio playing as usual in the studio with him. How could the sound be cut off, if it was playing in the studio?

Then embarrassment flooded over *her* as she realized what had happened. Unable to concentrate on her studies because of the contemporary music that had come on, she had turned off the radio and put on a quiet cassette tape instead. "Silent Night" was the last carol on the cassette tape. She had been studying so hard that she had forgotten this and had thought she was still listening to the radio.

Laughing out loud at her silliness, with red face she called the radio station again, explaining what had happened and apologizing for her mistake.

Then she went to bed. Evidently, the late night had taken its toll on her. Once more, studying would have to wait.

When grades came out, Lori looked at her list half-heartedly, expecting a C for speech class. There on the paper was an A+! Incredulous, Lori sought out her professor to ask him why.

"You were obviously frightened, but you knew your subject," he replied.

"Yes, but an A+? I could understand an A, but an A+?"

"I gave you an A+ because your improvement was phenomenal."

What a wonderful Christmas present!

Over the Net

"Goodbye, Sputnik. I love you!" My yellow tomcat purred and rubbed his head against me as I petted him.

"There are lots of mice in the barn, and the new owners will be here the day after tomorrow." I choked down a sob and tried to keep the tears out of my voice. "Mom says cats are good at taking care of themselves."

Looking directly into his yellow eyes, I whispered, "Jesus will take care of you." My heart was breaking.

> *All I could see was my last memory of Sputnik sitting in the driveway, watching us drive out of his life.*

"Michelle! Hurry up," Mother called from the driver's seat. Giving him one last caress, I ran to the car so Sputnik wouldn't follow me. I climbed into the back seat beside my younger brother and sister and shut the door. Hurriedly, I knelt on the seat and stared out the back window as the car began to move down the long driveway. Sputnik followed the car halfway down the driveway and then sat down. He watched as we turned left onto the road and drove away. Silent rivers flowed down my face. I turned around and sat down, pretending to look out the side window. All I could see was my last memory of Sputnik sitting in the driveway, watching us drive out of his life.

A few hours later, our little family walked across the tarmac at the Burlington airport to a waiting DC-3 airplane. Mother carried my sister, who had a leg brace. I followed, helping my little brother up the steps of the airplane. My ten-year-old brother Steve brought our huge carry-on bag. We had never flown in an airplane before, and the excitement of this new adventure helped me forget, for a while, the cat I had loved since he was a tiny four-week-old kitten.

Soon after the plane took off and leveled out, the stewardess stopped at our seats and spoke to my mother. "Would you like to move to first class? The seats are larger, and you will have more privacy there. There is one gentleman in the first-class section, and he said he would not mind if all of you joined him."

So we moved to the spacious and comfortable leather seats in first class. The gentleman greeted us warmly, and the stewardess brought us food and drinks. Steve and I spent hours playing games with our siblings and telling them stories. After they fell asleep, we watched dwarf houses and cars, like ants, crawl past on the ground far below us.

Unexpectedly, we heard the stewardess speaking to our mother. "Would the two older children like to go into the cockpit and watch the pilot fly the plane?" (This was way before security measures were needed as they are now.) Steve and I stared at each other in disbelief.

"Oh, thank you!" Mother turned to us. "Steve and Michelle, would you like to watch the pilot?"

"Yes," Steve enthusiastically responded. Timidly, I smiled and nodded my head. The stewardess opened the cockpit door and introduced us to the pilot, who sat in the left seat.

"Nice to meet you, Michelle and Steve," the pilot said. "Welcome! I have a boy and girl at home about your ages." He introduced us to the copilot.

Through narrow, horizontal windows Steve and I could see puffy white clouds in the sky. The pilot and copilot each had a steering wheel. Hundreds of switches and gauges covered the front of the cockpit and part of the ceiling. The pilot showed us how he made the plane go faster and slower, up and down. How exciting it was! Then the stewardess came to get us.

"In a short while we will begin our descent, so it's time to sit down and fasten your seatbelts," she explained.

When the plane landed in Cincinnati, we waited while all the other passengers exited the aircraft. Meanwhile, the pilot left the cockpit and made friends with my little sister and brother. He offered to carry my sister off the plane. She did not cry when he picked her up in his strong arms and carried her out of the airplane and down the steps before handing her to my mother.

"I hope you enjoy your new home," he said.

"Thank you," we responded. "And thank you for showing us how to fly," Steve added.

At the gate, our dad stood waiting with a big smile on his face. He hugged and kissed us. "I've missed you!" he said. "Wait until you see the house!"

The house in the suburbs Dad had chosen for us was a large English Tudor set on a double lot, surrounded by flowering trees and a rose garden. It was the most beautiful place in the cul-de-sac, which made leaving our twenty-seven-acre farm easier to bear.

However, going from a small-town school to a city school with 600 students was a different story. Always shy, I found myself rejected by all but one of the students in my fifth-grade class. And having to change rooms for each subject was so confusing. How I longed for my furry friend who loved me. I hoped he was okay, and that the new family loved him. I hoped he wasn't missing me.

"Mom, can we get a cat?" I asked as I cleared the dinner table one night.

"No, Michelle. The city is no place for a cat. He would get run over."

"But why couldn't he live with us in the house?"

"I don't want a litter box in the house. No, we won't be getting a cat."

In silence, I dried the dishes and put them away. But as I went to the room I shared with my sister, I prayed for a cat. I needed someone who would love me and rub his head on me and purr when I felt sad. My parents had adopted my little brother and sister a short time before we moved, and I was still adjusting to our larger family. I had lost the farm, my cat, my small town, my school, and all of my friends. I was having trouble making friends at this large school and in the neighborhood. Life in the suburbs of a big city was so foreign, so difficult to get used to. There were too many people. I needed a cat!

I asked a second time. The answer was still no. A few weeks later, I brought up the subject once more.

"No, you are not getting a cat, and don't ask me again." Mother's tone of voice let me know this was her final decision. I knew Mother meant what she said, and I gave up all hope. My parents bought us parakeets and hamsters, but although I enjoyed them, it just wasn't the same.

In gym class I learned how to play volleyball, a game I had never heard of before. It was fun, but I never could serve the ball over the net, which made the captains leave me until last when choosing their teams. Then my only friend at school deserted me and would not tell me why. I walked to my classes alone. No one spoke to me.

After each math lesson, my middle-aged math teacher read us a chapter from a book about Irish washerwomen. As she led us downstairs to the small gym for recess one day, she paused in the stairwell and gazed out the window at the beautiful rain-wet hills surrounding Cincinnati. With a sigh and with tears in her blue eyes, she told us they reminded her of the hills of Ireland. She was homesick. I knew how she felt.

Somehow I made it to Christmas vacation. Leaving school behind, I entered into the preparations with enthusiasm. This year I had a little sister and brother to share the fun and anticipation with. Steve and I helped them shop for presents for Mom and Dad. The four of us whispered and giggled as we wrapped our presents in secret. We made Christmas cookies and helped Dad put up the outdoor lights. Together we chose a Christmas tree and decorated it.

On Christmas Eve we hung our stockings from the fireplace mantel. Outside on the snowy sidewalk, a lamplighter walked by, lighting the gas lamps that cast a golden glow on the new fallen snow. We played games in front of the fireplace, popping corn in an old-fashioned wire basket over the fire. Life was good.

On Christmas morning we tiptoed downstairs to retrieve our bulging stockings and empty them onto our beds. As soon as Mom and Dad woke up, we flocked downstairs in our pajamas to the tree. Acting as Santa, I handed out one present at a time to each person, then opened mine. With a sigh I sat back in contentment as the phone rang and Mother went to answer it.

"Michelle, Santa accidentally left one of your presents at the neighbors' house," Mother called when she hung up the phone. "I'll go get it. Close your eyes, and don't open them until I tell you to."

In surprise, I obediently closed my eyes. I no longer believed in Santa Claus, but I played along for the sake of my new little brother and sister. What in the world could it be? I already had received what I wanted for Christmas. I couldn't imagine what the gift was, or why it would be next door.

In a few minutes, I heard the door open and close, and Mother's footsteps coming toward me. Suddenly something furry was purring in my lap. A cat! My eyes shot open. A young cat looked up at me with yellow eyes. His white fur was complemented by a few reddish-orange spots and his tail was ringed, like a raccoon's, with reddish-orange fur. He wore a red bow around his neck. The cat rubbed his head against my chest, and I hugged him, tears springing to my eyes.

"Hi, kit-ty! Hi, sweet kitty," I crooned. Filled with amazement and delight, I was aware of nothing but his energetic purring and rubbing against me as I petted him. It was mutual love at first sight.

"What are you going to name him?" Dad asked. I thought a moment.

"Well, he's a Christmas cat. I'll name him Jingles." Jingles put his front paws up on my chest and looked into my eyes, still purring.

"Jingles, do you like your name?" I asked him. He meowed, and we laughed.

The sound of an electric can opener came from the kitchen, and Jingles jumped down and ran toward it. I followed him and watched him eat hungrily. It was then that I remembered.

My prayer! I forgot I prayed for a cat, but God didn't forget! I felt warm and happy inside at this unexpected evidence of His love, and thanked Him with all my heart. *I think I can make it now, because You sent me a friend.*

Jingles was a perfect cat. He avoided the road. He meowed at the door to go out whenever the weather was good, and Mother allowed me to put a litter box in the basement for emergencies. We hung out together in the backyard by the rose garden, and at night he slept on my bed. When life became painful and I cried, Jingles put his face close to mine, purring and doing his utmost to comfort me. He was my best friend. Facing each day at school was not as difficult now, because I had Jingles to look forward to when I got home. He was just what I needed.

Then came the volleyball playoffs. It was my turn to serve the ball, for the winning point. Never yet had I been able to serve the ball over the net. My team members groaned audibly. The opposite team wore smiles of victory, anticipating their win. Perspiring with nervousness and dread, I felt that if I failed, my team members would forever hate me.

"Serve the ball," voices yelled, multiplying the stress. "Come on, serve the ball." The gym reverberated with impatient, taunting words. I rubbed my sweaty hands, one at a time, on my gym uniform. How I wished I could bury my face in Jingle's warm, comforting fur, and hear his loving purrs. I prayed, as I always did, but with more desperation. *Please, make it go over the net this time. Please!*

Suddenly I heard my captain's voice encouraging me. "You can do it, Michelle! You've got it! Come on, show them what you've got!"

Surprised, and grateful for the encouraging words, I held the ball on my left palm and smacked it with my right fist as hard as I could. Collectively we held our breath, watching the ball slowly sail in the direction of the net. *Farther, farther,* I begged. *Please!* The ball cleared the net, then fell straight down in front of the first row of players, who were too astonished to move before it hit the floor. *Thank You!* My team members cheered and lifted me up onto their shoulders. They carried me around, singing my praises. I had never been treated like that before. It was an amazing feeling, a good feeling.

Getting the ball over the net gave me confidence. From then on, I had no trouble serving the ball. Giving the game everything I had, I became one of my team's best players and spoke words of encouragement to my team members. The rest of the school still ignored me, but in gym class I felt accepted. And when I came home from school each day, Jingles was there for me, purring and telling me in his cat way that he adored me.

The days passed, and with Jingles' loving support I remained more confident. However, since my brother and I still struggled to fit in, our parents took us out of public school and enrolled us in a small church school. There we flourished with friends and beloved teachers we knew from church.

Jingles remained my best friend through high school. The night before I had to transfer to a large public school for my junior and senior years, Jingles was there, purring. He rubbed against me and made comforting "prrrrups" as I sat in the darkness on my bed, crying silently. I dreaded everything about public school. I did not want to feel like a misfit again. How I wished I could attend school with people who loved God, people who would respect me. Still, I knew that when I had finished expressing my fears and disappointment, I would dry my eyes and give it my best. I would submit to my parents and to God's will for my life. In my heart, I heard my heavenly Captain's voice encouraging me.

I gave it all I had. And I discovered that there are many kind-hearted, decent people in public school, even some who love God. This time I found it a little easier to make friends with students and teachers, and I felt mostly respected. And would you believe it—shy me won a poetry-reading contest with Edna St. Vincent Millay's poem "Renascence." In my senior year, I was chosen for induction into the National Honor Society. I guess this really shouldn't be that surprising. After all, God had sent a furry friend to help me "get the ball over the net." And every day I knew that when I got off the school bus, my best friend Jingles would be waiting for me.

Jingles moved with us from Cincinnati to Long Island, and spent a night in our car outside the Barbizon-Plaza Hotel in New York City without being stolen. For two summers he traveled to Camp Ella Fohs in Connecticut with us (my mother was camp nurse). He did not get lost in the woods or eaten by a coyote or a fisher. On every car trip, Jingles climbed up into the back window and slept until we stopped. On hot days when we ate at a restaurant, I hooked a leash to his collar and tied it to the underside of the car, where he waited for us in the shade.

Jingles truly was a miracle cat, surviving leukemia when the vet did not expect him to live. For weeks he could not keep any food or medicine down. He became emaciated, and his white fur turned yellow. My dear mother let me keep a litter box in my room. Finally, I gave in to Jingles' begging and let him outside, believing he wanted to die in secret. Jingles jumped off the steps into the flowerbed and ate mouthfuls of dirt, then walked shakily away. Calling out, "I love you, Jingles," I let him go, thinking I would never see him again. When he reappeared three days later, he was completely well, and ravenous. He wolfed down a bowl of cat food. Then, while we ate Thanksgiving dinner in the dining room, he leaped up onto the kitchen counter and began devouring the partially carved turkey. Mother was livid, but I thought Jingles deserved turkey. He was a survivor!

Rexie's Christmas

Rexie was a tiny baby Rex rat. She was black and white like an Oreo® cookie. Her fur was curly. Even her whiskers were curly.

Rexie lived in a cage at the pet store with her brothers and sisters. Every day Rexie's brothers and sisters grew bigger and fatter, but Rexie did not grow much. Her fur began to fall out. Rexie shivered with cold.

"Poor Rexie," said the girl who cleaned the cages. "You are so little. It is hard for you to get enough food. I will take you home with me for a while."

The girl fed Rexie special food. Rexie liked the food. She ate and ate. The girl kept Rexie nice and warm. Rexie began to feel better. Her fur grew back. Rexie grew bigger and bigger.

By Christmas time, Rexie was big and fat. The girl took her back to the pet store. But Rexie was unhappy. Her brothers and sisters were gone! Rexie was in the cage all by herself.

People came to the pet store to look at the animals. They looked at Rexie in her cage. Rexie felt afraid of the strange faces. There was no place to hide. Shaking with fear, she tried to hide under her exercise wheel.

One day a boy came into the store with his parents. He read Rexie's name on the cage. He looked at Rexie. Rexie shook with fear. Even her curly whiskers shook. She tried to hide under her exercise wheel.

"Poor Rexie," the boy said. "Don't be afraid. I won't hurt you." Rexie's nose wiggled and sniffed as she listened to his kind voice.

"I want to buy Rexie," the boy told his mother and father.

"Forrest, are you sure?" asked his mother. "Is this how you want to spend the money Aunt Beth sent you for Christmas? What about a bird or a hamster?"

"No," said the boy. "I want Rexie. I love her."

The boy bought Rexie with his Christmas money. He took Rexie home and put her into a big cage. Rexie stood just inside the cage door, shaking with fear.

Rexie's nose smelled food. She looked up. In a pretty dish she saw food. Rexie saw soft, warm bedding. She saw an exercise wheel. She saw a place to hide! Rexie ran toward the hiding place.

Suddenly Rexie stopped. Someone was in the hiding place!

Rexie's heart beat faster. Her nose wiggled and sniffed the air. Slowly she poked her nose and eyes through the door of the hiding place.

Inside was Rexie's sister!

Rexie and her sister sniffed each other's noses. They sniffed each other all over. Then they raced around the cage, playing. They ate food together. And when they were tired, they curled up together in the hiding place.

Rexie was very happy. She was not afraid anymore.

Have you ever moved to a new town or gone to a new school? New places and new people can be scary. Sometimes you may feel afraid, as Rexie did. But just like the boy in the story loved Rexie, Jesus loves you. He likes to do special things for you. Jesus will help you to be brave. And He will help you to make new friends, to feel loved, and not be afraid anymore.

The Late Great
Christmas Present

Mary hummed as she wrapped Christmas paper bright with snowmen around Ed's present and taped it shut. She cut a tiny square of wrapping paper, folded it in half, and wrote inside it, "For Ed, Love, Mary." Work at Ed's shop slowed down in the winter, making finances tight. They gave each other just one present, but Mary always managed to stuff a stocking with goodies for him. That had been her family's tradition. She smiled, anticipating Ed's present to her. It would be the latest book in Joe Wheeler's *Christmas in My Heart* series, and she could hardly wait to read it.

Setting the present aside, Mary began to wrap goodies for the stocking. She sighed. After Ed's present and goodies and a small donation to someone in need (as a gift for Jesus), she had only been able to squeeze out enough money to send *Creation Illustrated* magazine to her children and their families. Nothing special for the grandchildren. Well, almost nothing. She would keep it a secret, but she had a Noah's Ark sticker book for her littlest granddaughter. Mary would find a way to give it to her sometime after Christmas when no one was looking. The other grandkids were nearly grown up and would understand.

Mary sighed again, deeply. She would see none of them at Christmas—her beloved daughters, her precious grandchildren, her adored sons-in-law. Jody lived thousands of miles away and could not come east. Ariana lived barely an hour away, but she worked full time and her family kept her very busy. Mary rarely saw them. She drove down occasionally—when the car was working, and when Ed didn't need her. Now that she was older, driving the highway through the city stressed her greatly. And she usually felt disappointed as she drove home, because once again she had had no time with Ariana.

How she hungered for time alone with her daughter! Their life together had been cut short when Ariana turned fifteen. Upset by her parents' divorce and unable to face the verbal bullying at her small Christian school, Ariana had stopped going to school.

Mary still felt angry and indignant that *no one* had called Ariana to see if she was all right. Ariana's only friend had come by once to see what was wrong. But although Mary had gone to the school and explained to the teacher and the principal why Ariana was absent, they had never contacted Ariana or showed in any way that they cared.

Mary paused, her scissors in midair. An uncomfortable warmth flushed her cheeks and spread up the back of her neck. There had been times when she, too, in spite of her best intentions, had been so busy that she had neglected people who needed her loving words. How could she not forgive and forget the school's neglect of her daughter? It was past time to let it go. Taking a deep breath and exhaling slowly, she resumed cutting. Then she began to wrap a small package of roasted cashews, one of Ed's favorite treats.

After Ariana had been absent from school for two weeks, Mary had become desperate. Reluctantly, she had phoned Ariana's dad and explained the situation. "Will you talk to her and encourage her to go to school?" she asked him.

"Put her on the phone," he had commanded.

At the close of their short conversation, tears streamed down Ariana's cheeks and she clung to Mary. Wrapping paper and goodies forgotten, Mary relived the awful scene.

"Dad's coming to get me. I'm going to live with him. If I had known that it would end up with me leaving you, I would have acted differently," she cried.

Shocked, Mary wept with her. How do you spend your last half hour with your precious daughter? How she regretted involving Ariana's dad. Never had she dreamed that it would result in Ariana deciding to live with her father. And she had to let her go. Ariana was of legal age to choose which parent she wanted to live with. That terrible night, Mary cried herself to sleep, yearning for her daughter. She still had Jody, whom she also loved with all her heart, but there was a gaping hole in her life now where Ariana had been.

Mary reached for a tissue and wiped her eyes. She remembered, with embarrassment, that in a small way she had felt relief. At that time, she herself was trying to heal from years of emotional abuse. Raising a teenager alone had proved to be more than Mary could handle, even with counseling and attending a support group. Her frequent clashes with Ariana had been horrible, and Mary, more than once, had felt she couldn't go on anymore.

Most likely, Ariana felt the same way, Mary had reasoned at the time, feeling guilty. *That's probably why she went to live with her father.* Much later, Mary had learned the truth. On the phone Ariana's father had told her that she *had* to live with him—that if she stayed with her mother, the police would come and take her to a foster home. That was why she had left Mary.

Mary was not proud of what she had done next, but it was reality, and she had to face it. During Ariana's visits every other weekend, the changes Mary had seen in her were not for the better. On top of the emotional trauma she had already suffered, the pain of watching Ariana go downhill had driven Mary nearly insane. Fearing that Jody would follow in Ariana's footsteps, and feeling an overwhelming desire to distance herself from other family members who looked to her to fix their problems, Mary had done the unthinkable. She moved across the country, deserting Ariana during her teen years.

Mary still felt anguish in her heart, all these years later. If only she could do it over! If only she had not lost her grip on God's hand but had lived every moment for His smile. With His guidance, surely she could have resolved the issues differently.

Mary remembered how elated she had been when, returning to attend a family reunion in Vermont, she had found Ariana there. Reluctant to leave her at the end of the day, Mary had asked for a ride with the couple who had brought Ariana to the reunion. In the darkness of their van Ariana had laid her head, like a little girl, in Mary's lap, and Mary had stroked her hair until they had to say goodbye. That sweet half hour years earlier was the last quality time "alone" together that Mary could remember.

Mary wiped her eyes on her sleeve, then placed a cookie on a square of wrapping paper, folded it shut, and taped it.

At least Ariana had forgiven her, although they had not become close in the years since Mary had moved back. Their relationship felt awkward. Or maybe they didn't have a relationship. How could they, really, when they were never alone?

> *If only she could do it over! If only she had not lost her grip on God's hand but had lived every moment for His smile.*

On one recent visit, while the granddaughters chased each other loudly around the house, Ariana had confided that she, too, felt disappointed in Mary's visits.

"Everyone else gets time with you, except me. I feel left out."

She's hungering for time alone together, too, Mary realized, cutting another piece of wrapping paper. *But how do we accomplish it? Ariana is so busy.*

Mary recalled how, two weeks earlier, she had braved the trip to Ariana's, thinking she would finally have a day with her daughter. Erika had made plans with friends, and little Nancy intended to accompany her father to church while he played cello in a Christmas ensemble.

The anticipation bubbling up inside her made the drive feel easy. But upon arrival her hopes had been dashed. Both girls' plans had fallen through. Swallowing the lump in her throat, Mary had quickly adapted.

She loved spending time with her granddaughters. They could all make Christmas cookies together. Someday she would be alone with Ariana.

Ariana, visibly downcast, had buried herself in the computer room, while Erika sat engrossed in her iPod®. Mary had wished they could all be together and laugh often. And later, Ariana *had* emerged to decorate a couple of cookies with Mary and Nancy. That was Mary's happiest moment of the day.

Mary wrapped the last gift, filled Ed's stocking, and hid it in her bottom drawer. It was time to start supper. Ed would be home soon, and their Christmas Eve would begin.

On Christmas morning Ed surprised Mary with a stocking! Next, he handed her a large, odd-shaped gift. Her heart sank. It could not be the Christmas book. Uneasily, she undid the tape and pulled open the paper. Inside a slanted box, she found a beautiful pair of long blue oven mitts. Underneath was the Christmas book! Ed had bought her two gifts and wrapped them together to fool her.

With Ed absorbed in a computer crossword puzzle, Mary eagerly devoured the first story. But after the second one, she laid the book down and stared out the window, feeling lonesome.

If only I could have invited Ariana and John and the girls here for Christmas. I'm tired of celebrating Christmas without my family. I know it's my fault. After Jody was born, I decided we would create our own traditions instead of going to Mom and Dad's. I taught Ariana well.

Now I know how my parents must have felt on Christmas Day. The difference is, they always invited us the Sunday before Christmas to celebrate with the rest of the family. Our tiny apartment and John's allergy to cats does not allow us to do that. We cannot afford to take them to a restaurant for Christmas dinner. If only we lived in a big house.

An idea flashed into her mind.

"Ed! Can we invite Ariana and her family here this summer for a cookout? We could sit around the fire and eat and talk!"

"Yes, I guess that would work," Ed replied.

It wouldn't be Christmas, but it would be the next best thing. Bolstered by the expectation of a happy time to come, Mary spent the rest of Christmas content. Perhaps she would have a few minutes alone with Ariana! Somehow, sometime, God would make it happen.

Life resumed its hectic pace. Mary took down the nativity set and packed it away.

One morning the phone rang.

"Hello?"

"Hello, Mother; it's Ariana. I read on Facebook this morning that Ashley Drake died. I used to hang out with her daughter, Janine, when we were growing up."

"Oh, no! I heard she was in the nursing home, and I just sent her a card. Do you know why she died?"

"She had cancer. The funeral is on Friday at 11:00 in Lexington. I would like to go, but I don't want to go by myself. Are you planning to go?"

"I didn't realize she was that sick. Yes, I would like to go, but I don't want to go by myself, either. Do you want to go together?" Mary held her breath.

"Sure. I'll drive over and pick you up. I have to get back to work now. See you Friday about nine."

"All right. I'm looking forward to seeing you."

"I'm looking forward to seeing you, too!"

Mary practically hugged herself at the thought of seeing her daughter, *alone*! Over the next few days as she grieved for her friend, she wondered how Ariana was faring. In spite of her sorrow, she could not help feeling a little excited. She hoped their ride together would go well.

Ariana looked attractive and professional in her work attire. On their way to the car, they met the neighbors coming in.

"Having some mother-daughter time, huh?"

"We're going to a funeral." Mary could not help beaming.

"Oh, we're sorry."

"It's all right. It's the first time Ariana and I have been alone together in years, and I can't stop smiling!"

To Mary's surprise, the conversation flowed effortlessly as though they had never been apart. She found that they thought alike on most subjects they discussed. The sad funeral, paradoxically, felt happy as they glanced sideways at each other and afterward observed each other's interactions with the deceased's family and friends from Ariana's childhood.

The ride back to Mary's apartment seemed way too short.

"I know you have to get to work, but do you have time to come in for a minute?" Mary asked, hoping.

"I can spend a few minutes," Ariana agreed. Mary felt a little nervous sitting with Ariana in the living room with no one else around. She gave

Ariana a shy smile, and right away thought of something to ask her. They chatted like old friends. Glancing at the clock a while later, Mary felt concerned. It was almost one o'clock, and Ariana had not eaten breakfast. She could not send her on her way without lunch. But today was shopping day, and Mary had nothing in the house to feed her.

What should I do? I don't want her to faint on the way to work.

Instantly, the words spilled from her mouth. "Would you like to get a grinder* at Jon's Pizza? I'll pay for yours." Surely she and Ed would make it through the month with this unexpected expense. She would trust God.

"I'd love to!" Jon's grinders had been Ariana's favorite food while growing up. "But you don't have to pay for me. I have hardly ever given *you* anything." Ariana looked ashamed.

"You *have* done a lot for me," Mary reassured her. "Remember when I lived out west and you paid for my plane ticket to visit you and your family, and took me out to eat, and to the zoo, and to get ice cream? I want to do something for *you*," Mary insisted.

They went out to the car and drove a mile down the road to Jon's. The years had not changed the small pizza parlor.

"You go first," Mary said, scanning the menu.

"I'll have a vegetarian turkey grinder with green peppers, no onions, please."

"And I'll have a vegetarian turkey grinder with green peppers, no cheese, please," Mary ordered. She looked at Ariana and they both laughed. It was just like old times.

They sat opposite each other in a small booth by the window. Ariana savored her first bite slowly, with a huge sigh of pleasure. Mary bit hungrily into her grinder, then closed her eyes groaning, "M-m-m-m-m!" The taste was as mouthwatering as it had always been. They smiled at each other's enjoyment. In between mouthfuls, their conversation continued.

When Ariana pulled into Mary's parking spot, Mary gave her a lingering hug.

"Thank you for spending extra time with me. It means more than you know. I love you very much."

Ariana's reply was music to Mary's ears. "Work can wait. I love you, too."

---

* A submarine sandwich, also called a hoagie.

Mary watched and waved until the car was out of sight. She felt lighter than air as she floated back to the apartment, her face alight with joy and awe at what had just happened. Closing the door, she cried tears of happiness.

"Lord, Thank you! Thank you for the wonderful, amazing, fantastic present you just gave me! You gave me a late Christmas present, didn't you? You are so awesome! And I believe it is just the beginning of many more good times to come."

Puppy Finds a Home

Puppy was lost. All day long under the hot desert sun she had walked and walked, looking for a home. Her feet were tired and sore, and she was very hungry.

By suppertime she stood outside a gate. Inside the fence was a small house. Through a big window Puppy could see a lady and a girl. Puppy sniffed the air. It smelled like supper!

Puppy sat down outside the gate and waited.

The lady came outside. "Hello, Puppy!"

Puppy stood politely and wagged her tail, begging with her eyes. When Puppy's tail wagged, her whole body wagged. Puppy didn't wiggle; she waggled. The white tip of her tail flashed back and forth like a light.

"You poor puppy! You must be so thirsty on such a hot day. Your black coat soaks up the sun's rays." The lady brought a bowl of cool water, and Puppy drank thirstily.

"I'm sorry, Puppy, but you cannot have any food, because I do not want you to stay. We have four cats. You need to go find your home."

Puppy sighed. She lay down in front of the gate and slept.

In the morning, the lady and the girl came outside. The girl carried some books and a lunchbox. Puppy waggled, then sniffed the lunchbox.

"Puppy, you're still here!" exclaimed the lady. "You need to go find your home." The lady and the girl got into the car and drove away.

Puppy walked down the fence, looking for breakfast. She saw two cats, but they did not want to be friends. She walked to a small trailer behind the house and sat down. She waited for a while, but no one came out. Just then she heard the car. Puppy trotted back around the corner of the fence.

"Oh, Puppy, you're still here," the lady sighed. "Now I will have to take you to the shelter. I can't keep you and I don't want you to be hungry. Come on, Puppy." She opened the car door.

Puppy obediently jumped into the car. She sat royally on the back seat, her curly white chest gleaming against her black coat. The lady glanced thoughtfully at Puppy in the rearview mirror as she drove. The car went slower and slower. Finally the car stopped on the side of the road. The lady turned her head and looked at Puppy.

"Puppy," she said. "You have good manners. You do not bark or whine. You are loyal even when you are not fed. I cannot take you to the shelter. You are too good a dog."

The lady turned the car around and drove back home. She let Puppy out and opened the gate.

"Come on, Puppy," she said. "You can live here."

Puppy waggled happily through the gate. The white tip on her tail flashed back and forth like a light. The lady went inside the house. Puppy sat down and waited.

"Here you go, Puppy." The lady placed a bowl of food on the porch. Puppy waggled and smiled to thank the lady. Then she ate.

The girl seemed glad to see Puppy there when she came home from school. She spoke kindly to Puppy and petted her. Puppy waggled, and the tip of her tail flashed back and forth like a light.

Puppy liked living at the little house. She liked to sit in the front yard and watch people and cars go by. She liked the lady and the girl, and she could tell that they liked her. Puppy liked the cats, but they did not like her. She tried to play with them, but they would not play with her.

Sometimes the lady and the girl took Puppy to visit their friend Blake, who lived on a ranch. Puppy loved going to the ranch. She made friends with the ranch dogs, and together they ran happily through the desert chasing rabbits. She made friends with the cattle and the horses, and even with the chickens. Puppy liked not being stuck inside the fence around the little house. She liked Blake, too.

Puppy grew and grew. Her tail fur grew long, and hung down. Now her tail did not flash like a light. It waved like a flag. But Puppy's body still waggled when she was excited or happy.

"Why, Puppy!" exclaimed the lady one day. "You are growing up! Now I know what kind of dog you are. You are a border collie! And you are not a little puppy anymore. I don't think we should call you Puppy. We will call you Puppy Dog."

Puppy Dog waggled happily and smiled. Her tail waved grandly, like a flag.

The rainy season came. Day after day it rained. The dirt inside the fence around the little house turned to mud.

Puppy Dog was unhappy. She stood on the porch and looked out at the rain and the mud. She did not want to stay on the porch. She wanted to run and play and look at the people and the cars going by. So she did. Her fur got soaked. Her feet got muddy. Mud splashed onto her white chest and onto all the long hairs hanging from her tail. Puppy Dog was cold and miserable.

The next day Blake came. He saw Puppy Dog standing all wet, muddy, cold, and unhappy in the rain and in the mud.

"Poor Puppy Dog," said Blake. "Puppy Dog says she wants to go home with me to the ranch for a few days."

"All right," agreed the lady. So Puppy Dog went to the ranch with Blake.

Puppy Dog rode in the back of the pickup truck. She moved from side to side, grinning, loving the feel of the wind in her face, and looking at everything she could see.

The dirt road to the ranch was very muddy from the rain. As the truck clawed its way up the hill, Puppy Dog leaned out to see where they were going. Suddenly the truck slid and Puppy Dog fell out onto the muddy road and lay still. The truck continued up the hill and out of sight. Then there was silence.

Slowly, Puppy Dog stood up. Her black fur coat was brown with cold, wet mud. Puppy Dog looked around. She did not know where she was. She could not see the little house. She could not see the ranch or the truck or her doggie friends. Puppy Dog felt scared. She scooted into some grease-wood bushes beside the road and hid there. Just then the truck came back down the hill, but it did not stop. Puppy Dog listened as the truck went farther and farther away. Then she could not hear it anymore. Puppy Dog shivered.

Suddenly Puppy Dog heard the truck again, far away. Her ears perked up. She heard the truck stop. Then she heard Blake's voice, but she could not hear what he was saying. She heard the truck start up again. It sounded like it was coming closer! It stopped, and she heard Blake calling.

"Puppy Dog! Puppy Dog!"

In a moment the truck started again. The truck came closer and closer. It stopped right near the greasewood bushes where Puppy Dog was hiding.

"Puppy Dog!" Blake called. "Puppy Dog!"

Puppy Dog jumped up and ran to him.

"Puppy Dog, there you are! I am so sorry," Blake said in a soft voice, petting her muddy head. He opened the tailgate.

"Jump in, Puppy Dog. Try not to lean out so far."

This time Puppy Dog was careful. When they got to the ranch, Blake took Puppy Dog into the bunkhouse and put her into the shower. Puppy Dog hated the shower! She kept trying to get out, and Blake kept pushing her back in until all the mud was washed off. Then he began to dry her with some towels. Puppy Dog shook, and the rest of the water went flying all over the bathroom and all over Blake. Poor Blake! Puppy Dog was clean and almost dry, but Blake was wet, muddy, cold, and unhappy!

Suddenly Puppy Dog heard something outside the door. Her friends! She raced to the door and whined. Blake opened the door, and Puppy Dog waggled out, greeting her friends with a bark and her tail waving. They all ran happily through the desert, chasing rabbits.

The next day Puppy Dog sat beside Blake on the porch.

"You know, Puppy Dog," Blake said as he stroked her clean fur, "Puppy Dog is such a long name to say when I'm calling you. How about P.D.?"

P.D. thumped her tail on the porch. Then she lay down and rolled over so Blake could rub her belly. She closed her eyes and sighed with pleasure.

On Christmas Day, the lady and the girl showed up at the ranch.

"P.D., we have visitors!" Blake called. P.D. waggled all over when she saw who it was. Her tail waved grandly.

"Puppy Dog! How are you?" they asked. "We are so glad to see you! We brought you a present." P.D. whined excitedly and pushed her nose into their hands.

The girl gave P.D. a present wrapped in Christmas paper. It smelled delicious. She lay on the porch, held her present down with both paws, and ripped open the paper with her teeth. She gobbled up her favorite treat. Then she jumped up and sniffed their hands for more, waggling.

Blake stood watching them with a smile on his face. After a minute he said, "Puppy Dog says she prefers to be called P.D. Isn't that right, P.D.?"

P.D. grinned and kept on waggling. Joyfully she trotted before them as they hiked up the dirt road to the windmill, her tail waving proudly like a flag on the Fourth of July. As they neared the ranch house, her doggie friends came running to join the fun. P.D. watched the lady and the girl climb up the windmill and look down at her. She barked at them to be careful. The lady and the girl climbed down and scooped water from the huge tank into their cowboy hats. PD and her friends lapped the water thirstily.

The dogs raced off to hunt for rabbits. They came back with their tongues hanging out, just as the people crossed over the cattle guard in front of the bunkhouse. P.D.'s doggie friends went home to take a nap. P.D. napped on the cool front porch.

After Christmas dinner, the lady asked, "When are you going to bring Puppy Dog, I mean, P.D., back home?"

"Uh-h-h-h-h, P.D. says she wants to stay here at the ranch," Blake said slowly. "Right, P.D.?"

P.D. thumped her tail on the porch floor and grinned. Her grin ended in a noisy yawn.

"Well, here she has room to run and friends to play with," said the lady. "And you certainly seem to understand her needs better than I do. We have missed her, but we do have four cats. I think the ranch is better for her. Let's see what P.D. wants."

The lady opened the car door. "Do you want to go home with us, P.D.?"

P.D. sat down. She did not jump in.

"Come on, P.D.," called the lady. P.D. just sat there. She thumped her tail on the ground and whined.

"Well, it looks like P.D. has made her choice," said the lady. "Is it okay with you?" she asked the girl. "After all, she is your dog."

"It's okay. P.D. is happy here. I miss her, but this is the best place for her. We can come and visit her."

The lady and the girl petted P.D. goodbye. "You come and see us, okay, P.D.?" they said.

P.D. barked goodbye as they drove away. Then she trotted back to the porch, sat down, and looked up at Blake.

Blake knelt in front of P.D. and stroked her head and ears lovingly with both hands.

"Well, P.D.," he said, "I guess it's you and me now, girl. This is your home. You can stay as long as you like. Merry Christmas!"

P.D. thumped her tail loudly on the porch floor. She loved the ranch and all of her doggie friends. She loved Blake, and he loved her. She laid her head on Blake's arm, leaned against him, and sighed with happiness.

Suddenly, her ears perked up and she raised her head. Her friends were coming! With a joyous bark she ran to greet them, waggling all over, her tail waving. In excited little barks she told them the glad news. Then together they raced off through the desert, chasing rabbits.

Home for Christmas

Home for Christmas! Joy gave my heart wings as the shuttle bus sped down the highway to the airport. It had been several years since my younger daughter, Jasmine, and I had been able to get home to New England for Christmas. And what is Christmas without family? This Christmas was especially exciting because I would see my little newborn granddaughter for the first time!

I glanced over at Jasmine. Her eyes held excitement in spite of dark circles that revealed her need of a rest from her junior year in high school. I knew my eyes reflected that excitement, although the slump of my body revealed total exhaustion. This had been my first semester as dean of girls at a boarding academy, and the semester had been really tough.

At the airport we checked our bags and successfully made it through security. As the airplane reached cruising altitude, Jasmine fell asleep, and I was left alone with my thoughts.

Thinking back over the previous six years, I felt both pleasure and pain. These had been some of the happiest years of my life, and yet, at the same time, very unhappy. Deep inside me, I had known I was not living right, and I had made sporadic efforts to change. God had continued to reach out to me, showing me He loved me and was still there for me. Through many different experiences, He had tried to teach me to trust Him.

God had taken care of Jasmine and me on our move to New Mexico and on the many bus, car, and plane trips we had made back and forth to New England. He had protected us in the New York City bus station while we waited for our connecting bus. When we had arrived in Worcester, Massachusetts, at 11:00 p.m. and no one was there to meet us, He already had a solution. A kindhearted taxi driver offered to drive us the twenty miles to my sister's house for the small amount of money I had with me.

God had been there for me when Jasmine's youth group spent a day at the Rio Grande River. As Jasmine swam in the murky water, a branch from a submerged tree ripped through her upper lip and sliced her gum. At the emergency room, we had to wait an hour and a half for an orthodontic surgeon to arrive. Unable to reach anyone I knew, and filled with anxiety and fear for my daughter, I reached out to God and found He

Driving to my friends' ranch, I walked far out among the mesquite and greasewood bushes where no one could see or hear me. Sobs wrenched my body as I looked up toward heaven.

was there. In that quiet room while I comforted Jasmine, God filled my heart with His peace, and I knew everything would be all right. It was. I made it through without any human being to depend upon. The insurance paid for all expenses, and Jasmine's scar became barely noticeable.

These answers to prayer, and the realization that I had been miserable inside for some time, brought everything to a climax one day in the desert. Driving to my friends' ranch, I walked far out among the mesquite and greasewood bushes where no one could see or hear me. Sobs wrenched my body as I looked up toward heaven.

From the wretchedness of my heart I cried, "God, I can't do this anymore! I am *so miserable*. But every time I try to break away and live the way You want me to, I keep failing. I can't do it! I give up! Will You help me, God? *You* have to do it; I can't."

Under a mesquite bush, I knelt on the sand. "God, here I am, with all my imperfections and sin. I've made a mess of my life. Will You take me and make me what You want me to be? I promise to serve You with my whole heart. Open the way before me. Provide for Jasmine and me. You have been showing us that we can trust You. I choose to trust You now. Change me and guide me. I give You permission."

God *had* helped me, by opening the way for me to begin a new life as the dean of girls at an academy four states away. It certainly was not easy, especially when my heart was aching, but I knew I was where God wanted me to be. Life would get better.

The droning of the plane's engines made me sleepy. I leaned my tired head against Jasmine's golden hair and caught some much-needed sleep until the flight attendant asked us to prepare for the descent.

Glancing at my watch, I knew it would be a miracle if we made it to our next flight in time. As soon as the door opened and we could exit the plane, Jasmine and I dashed up the jet bridge to the terminal. Frantically, we searched for a monitor screen that would show us the gate number for our flight.

My eyes raced through the departures to Boston. As *Cancelled* jumped out at me, my heart nearly stopped beating.

"Cancelled? Why? What are we supposed to do now?" In dismay I looked at Jasmine. Was that fear I saw shadowing her eyes? I needed to be strong, for her.

"I guess we'd better go to the gate and see what we can find out," I decided. We shouldered our carry-on bags and hurried to the gate. A long line of people stood in front of the flight representative, and we joined them. Finally, we reached the front of the line.

"There is a snowstorm in Boston," the representative informed us. "I can get you on another flight, but it won't be until morning."

Inwardly I groaned. Staff at the struggling academy received a small stipend and I did not have money for a hotel room. We would have to spend the night in the Newark airport, which could be dangerous. Staying up all night did not thrill me, either, since I was already exhausted. And we would lose part of a day with family—at Christmas.

After booking a flight for early the next morning, we explored the airport. At about 9:30 p.m., beside the soothing music of an indoor water-fall, we ate our lunch leftovers, watching passengers hurry by. I assured

Jasmine that God would take care of us, but she must have heard fear in my voice.

"Mom, remember when I cut my lip swimming, and God helped us through it? He will help us through this, too."

Gratefully, I smiled at my daughter with tears in my eyes. What a blessing she was to me!

"You're right! And remember how He took care of us at the bus station in New York City? He will be with us."

We brushed our teeth, then searched for a place in the terminal to spend the night. Instinctively, I looked for a well-lit place where there were several other people. We sat down across from a sweet-looking white-haired couple. Jasmine spread out on the seats with her pillow and soon fell asleep, but I sat upright with our carry-on bags between my feet. Silently, I reached out to the One who had always taken care of us.

Lord, I've never been in this situation before. Will you help me stay awake? I don't want anyone to steal our luggage or hurt us. Please protect us with your holy angels. I'm trusting You.

A few hours dragged by, and Jasmine slept on. After a while, I found my eyelids closing and my head nodding. *Father, please help me. I can't do this anymore. I am so tired.*

Across the hall a door opened and a woman stepped out. Scrutinizing the group of passengers, she approached us and stopped in front of me. Her uniform logo was that of the airline we were to fly on.

"Would you and your daughter like a hotel room? We keep a hotel room for the flight attendants, and it is not occupied," she explained. "You are welcome to use it. Our airport shuttle van will take you there and bring you back in the morning in time for your flight."

"Oh, yes, we would! Thank you so much," I replied.

"Just go through that door over there, and someone will help you." She continued on her way.

Quickly I roused Jasmine and we hurried across the hallway and through the door. The lady inside made arrangements for us, and we rushed out of the terminal to the waiting shuttle. The friendly driver stashed our luggage as we climbed into the van. After a couple of stops to let the other passengers off, we arrived at the hotel.

"The van will pick you up out front at 5:00 a.m.," the driver said as he handed us our luggage. "Have a good night."

Inside, the desk clerk heard our story and gave us our key. "I will call you at 4:30 a.m.," she assured us.

We had only a few hours to sleep, but oh, how good that bed felt! Before we slept, I had a short talk with the One who always takes care of us.

"You are so wonderful! Thank You. I know You will protect us and help us get back to our airplane on time. Good night."

We arrived back at the terminal in time and made our flight. My heart sang with gratitude and joy as we threw ourselves into the waiting arms of our family. Once again, God had been faithful, and we were finally home. As I held in my arms the most beautiful baby in the world, I gratefully remembered another beautiful baby—the One who grew up to take our sins and give us new life. The One we can trust to bring us Home.

That Kind of Love

Charley sat on the screened porch, listening to the giant pine's branches swaying in the wind. His heart throbbed with the wonder of his father's love. Deep inside, he had always known his dad loved him. But tonight— tonight he knew beyond a shadow of a doubt. His fingers rubbed the rough bandage on his forearm, and he winced.

What a man his dad was! Admiration rose up in his chest and nearly took his breath away. Charley shook his head in amazement at what had just taken place. But it really wasn't unusual. It was just the way Dad had always been. Charley's surroundings faded as his mind went back in time.

Dad was taking all nine of them for a walk while Mother rested. Dad led the way, carrying the new baby, while the bunch of them, by twos and threes, fell into line behind him. They crossed the dirt road and passed through the meadow, over the railroad tracks and on to Lake Shaftsbury. They had rounded the south end of the lake and entered a stand of pines and firs when a freak storm broke upon them. Gale force winds felled trees around them.

"Stay close behind me and do what I do!" Dad commanded. He scanned the trees, noting in which direction each tree began to fall. Still carrying the baby, he sprang out of the way, his progeny bounding behind. Dad brought them safely through the woods, with only his eyeglasses brushed off by a falling evergreen. Arriving at home, they found two boards from the sawmill across the valley lying in their front yard.

Another snapshot of his father's character came to Charley's mind. He and his younger brothers, Joe and Andrew, were watching Dad use the cordwood saw. Suddenly, Dad cut his hand badly. No swear words or hollering came from his lips. At the sight of his dad bleeding, Andrew began to cry.

"Don't cry, Andrew," Dad soothed. "Everything will be all right." He sent the boy to his mother for comfort and calmly wrapped his hand in a handkerchief. Then he drove himself to the hospital, accompanied by Charley and Joe.

That brought to mind Dad's constant cheerfulness and positive outlook, and the twinkle in his blue eyes—until Uncle Sam had called him up for the Korean conflict. Charley still remembered the sorrow in Dad's eyes as they gathered in the farmhouse parlor for prayer. Dad prayed for each one of them, and the strong hug he gave Charley assured him of his love. They surrounded Dad as he walked out to the dirt road, satchel in hand, and headed down the road to do his duty for his country. The house seemed like a tomb for the next few days until, unexpectedly, those twinkly blue eyes reappeared! How thrilled they were to find that Uncle Sam had released him! Again they gathered in the parlor, this time to thank God for Dad's safe and rapid return.

Many people admired Dad. His ingenious mind made him a jack-of-all-trades, and folks at church and in the community often called on him when something needed fixing. Dad always seemed to relish an opportunity to serve others. His keen eyes and ears were quick to notice when someone needed food or firewood. What an example he was to the boys!

The breeze blew the acrid odor of singed flannel up into Charley's nostrils. He stood up and carefully removed his shirt. Going over to the bureau, he took out a clean flannel shirt, making sure not to dislodge the candle that sat on top of the bureau. Gingerly, he slid his injured arm into a sleeve, then his other arm, and buttoned up his shirt. He sat down again, lost in thought.

He had seen the love and pride in Dad's eyes when the gang dressed up for church. He could feel it in the way Dad squeezed his shoulder as he passed by. He had watched Dad's tired eyes light up after a long day at work when they all ran to hug him. Yes, he knew he was loved, but everything paled in comparison to what had just happened. For, tonight—tonight Dad had saved his life! Charley relived the scenes in his mind.

They were eating Christmas dinner. The electricity had been out for five days, cut off by a December blizzard. Candlelight revealed a groaning table, laden with the delicious results of Grandma and Mother's loving labors. Engrossed in the happy chatter, Charley reached for the bowl of mashed potatoes, forgetting the candle between him and the bowl. Its eager flame leapt high and ignited his flannel shirt sleeve.

Screaming, Charley jumped up, thrashing his arms. The flames shot even higher, devouring his sleeve and licking hungrily at the tender skin of his arm.

Quick as a flash, his six-foot-two dad vaulted over the corner of the table and smothered the fire with his large hands. Wrapping Charley in his embrace, Dad held him close for a moment, then examined Charley's arm to determine how awfully he had been burned. The skin was badly reddened, but not black. Mother buttered his arm and wrapped it in a clean dish towel.

> *He had been so caught up in his own trauma and in his dad's love that he had not realized his dad's danger.*

A cold blast of wind brought Charley out of his reverie. He was shivering. The pain was beginning to come again. Charley took the candle from the dresser and re-entered the house to spend what was left of Christmas with his family. That night he slept little, painfully aware of his injured flesh.

In the morning, his dad walked all the way into town to buy burn ointment and bandages for Charley's arm. With his own hands, he spread the ointment on the huge blisters that now protruded from Charley's arm. As he wrapped the arm with a bandage, he gently reminded Charley that movement increases the oxygen supply to a fire, and that the best way to put out a fire is to remain calm and cover the fire so that no oxygen can get to it.

Charley thought that surely was true. Dad had covered the fire with his bare hands and snuffed it out. *Dad's hands! How are Dad's hands?* His anxious heart nearly skipped a beat.

"Dad! Were your hands burnt? Are you okay?" he choked. Mentally he chastised himself for not having thought of that sooner. He had been so caught up in his own trauma and in his dad's love that he had not realized his dad's danger.

Dad held his hands with the palms up, for Charley to inspect.

"Don't worry, Charley," he said. "By God's grace, I escaped harm." His eyes twinkled.

Charley's pent-up breath rushed out in a sigh of relief. Tears pooled in the corners of his eyes. How precious Dad was! Never would he want to be the cause of his dad's hurting. The rest of the boys felt the same way, he was sure. All of them loved nothing more than to be in Dad's presence.

To handle the pain when the bandage was changed, Charley concentrated on his dad's loving self-sacrifice. In his mind's eye he again saw his dad leaping over the table and putting himself in danger to save his son's life. He recalled how his dad had walked to town and back, and cared for his burned arm with his own hands.

Something nagged at him. He had heard the phrase "loving self-sacrifice" before, but where? It had not been very long ago. Now he remembered—it was in the pastor's Christmas sermon. After describing the incredible love of God in coming to earth as a baby and living as one of us, the pastor had reminded them that He had taken their sins upon Himself and died for each one of them.

Jesus had loved him enough to put His own life in danger and die for him! Charley understood it now as he never had before. In effect, Jesus' love had saved him from the flaming death of hell fire just as truly as his dad's love had saved him from a flaming death on Christmas night. But Dad's dear hands had not been injured, whereas Jesus' hands and body had been wounded and scarred. Jesus had given his life, and Charley knew his dad would have done the same for him, if necessary.

That night, under the sighing branches of the pine tree, a great resolve welled up inside him. He vowed that their love would not go unappreciated. He would be that kind of man, too. He would bravely and courageously fulfil every duty. He would live cheerfully, honorably, and generously. By God's grace, he would accomplish it. For as long as God would give him breath, he would do his utmost to live that kind of love, for God, for his family, and for all humanity.

Charley's burn, tended by his father's loving hands, healed without a scar.

Love Was There

Erin's voice startled her from a sound sleep. "Mom," she called so weakly, Heather could barely hear her.

"I'll be right there!" Heather struggled into her robe and slippers and hurried into Erin's room. "What's wrong, Sweetie?" She couldn't resist the childhood endearment even though Erin was a junior in high school.

"I don't feel good."

Heather laid her hand on Erin's forehead. She had a fever. And her breathing didn't sound right. Leaning down, Heather laid her ear on Erin's chest and listened. Her heart sank.

"Oh-h, I think you have pneumonia again. On the day before Christmas! I'm so sorry. I'll get some hot towels."

Heather went down the hall to the kitchen. Getting out a large pot, she filled it with water and set it on the stove to boil. Meanwhile, she prepared a pan of ice water, put a washcloth in it, and set it on Erin's bedside table. From the linen closet Heather took three large bath towels and three medium towels. When the water came to a boil, she lifted the ends of a medium towel and submerged the middle of it in the boiling water. As she raised it from the water, she twisted the ends, wringing the water out. She placed the steaming towel onto an open bath towel and folded its sides in over the wet towel. Grabbing it by the ends, she ran to the bedroom and laid the hot pack on Erin's chest for three minutes.

After a moment, she slid her hand under the hot pack to make sure it was not burning Erin. Hurrying back to the kitchen, she placed another towel into the boiling water, and by the time she had prepared the hot pack and entered the bedroom, it was time to remove the first pack.

"This is going to be cold." Erin gasped as Heather scrubbed her chest rapidly and briefly with the washcloth she had wrung out of ice water. Then Heather laid the second hot pack on Erin's chest while she prepared a third. She did that three times a day.

Most of the time Erin slept. The house was quiet! Heather spent Christmas Day alone with the silence, in between treatments. The gifts remained in the closet, unwrapped.

For a week Heather battled the pneumonia with hot packs, fruit juices, hot teas, and soup. By New Year's Eve, Erin was on the mend. Heather brought Erin her unwrapped presents and sat on the bed while she exclaimed over them.

They had missed Christmas, but it would come again.

Erin graduated from high school and went away to college. Heather could hardly wait until Christmas break when Erin would be home for two weeks.

A couple of days before Christmas, Erin arrived, and Heather, worn out from their recent move and her new job, promptly came down with the flu. Erin spent the first week of her vacation caring for her mother with as much love as Heather had cared for her. She spent Christmas Day alone while her mother slept.

By New Year's Eve Heather had recovered, but the presents remained unwrapped in the closet.

About nine o'clock, Erin went to bed. Heather sat slumped in the rocking chair, feeling sad that Erin had missed Christmas again. And sad that *she* had missed Christmas. For the beauty, the surprise, the excitement, the magic of Christmas comes only once a year. Heather would give

Erin her presents, but it wouldn't be the same. Christmas was over, and the country had moved on into celebrating New Year's.

She rocked in the stillness until a lightning thought brought her to an abrupt halt. New Year's was a holiday, too, exactly a week after Christmas. Why couldn't she pretend that tonight was a week earlier, and it was Christmas Eve? Energized with excitement, Heather jumped up.

I can cut down a pine tree in the woods! It will be scary, but God will help me. And we can listen to Christmas records. We are not expecting anyone tomorrow, so we can celebrate with a special meal and read the Christmas story from the Bible like we always do. She'll be so surprised! She'll think I'm silly, but she'll love it!

Heather put on her coat, boots, and mittens, and grabbed the handsaw and the flashlight. Stepping out into the darkness, she closed the door gently behind her. The sky was alight with stars, and there was a brighter one that reminded her of the star over the manger where Baby Jesus lay. The night seemed hushed, as if waiting for something.

Noiselessly she made her way around to the front of the large farmhouse and crossed the road. Entering the orchard, she lifted the flashlight to scan between the apple trees to make sure she wasn't about to startle a deer. Or, rather, to make sure no deer's alarmed snort would startle her. Soon she left the orchard for the path through the woods, flashing the light on the ground and around the woods. No deer eyes reflected the flashlight's glow. No grouse exploded loudly into the air from the ground before her. About 100 feet in, she came to a small clearing where pine saplings crowded one another. Then she realized that the tree would have to be small enough for her to carry it along with the saw and still be able to aim the flashlight in the right direction.

It was unnerving alone in the woods at night. With her flashlight, Heather moved around through saplings taller than herself, searching for a smaller one. Every pine she saw was too large.

Maybe I should walk farther. She felt as if eyes were watching her. The hairs stood up on the back of her neck.

Are there bears in these woods? No one knows where I am. Maybe this was a foolish idea. She turned and beat a hasty retreat back down the path and through the orchard.

There's the barn. I'm safe. She felt downcast. Her search had been fruitless. Now what could she do?

A sudden noise made her heart thump in her chest. Something was there! Trembling, she turned her flashlight toward the barnyard. Relief flooded over her as its beam revealed her twelve-year-old neighbor boy.

"Tighe! You scared me!"

"I'm sorry! What are you doing?"

"I was trying to find a Christmas tree."

"A Christmas tree! What for?"

"I had the flu, and we couldn't celebrate Christmas, so we're having Christmas on New Year's. But I couldn't find a tree small enough," she explained.

"Lafe was here yesterday, and he bulldozed up a tree. It's right over there. Shine the light."

Tighe walked over and picked a small pine out of the snow. Clumps of frozen snow encased the needles on one side.

"It's perfect! I mean, it will be when the snow and ice melt."

"I'll cut off the roots for you."

Tighe took the saw and Heather held the flashlight while he sawed off the trunk. "I left enough to fit into a tree stand," he said as he stood up and handed her the tree.

"Thank you, Tighe! Merry Christmas!"

He laughed as she excitedly ran back to the house. She had her tree!

In the kitchen, Heather set the tree in a bucket of stones gleaned from their rock collection. Then she went into the living room and put on some Christmas music. Getting out the Christmas box, she lit one of the candles and set it in some evergreens on the piano. Lovingly, she set up the nativity nearby—the very one she had set up as a child. Then she went upstairs and retrieved the presents and wrapping paper from her closet. As she cut, folded and taped, chuckles erupted at the thought of Erin's surprised face in the morning. Humming along with the carols, she pretended it was snowing outside.

When the gifts were wrapped, she carried the tree into the living room. After decorating it with colored lights and cherished ornaments, she placed the larger presents underneath. Finally, she filled Erin's stocking. Carrying it in her arms, she padded quietly up the stairs to Erin's room and paused at her door, listening. Erin was breathing deeply. Soundlessly Heather crept into the room.

Oh, what if I drop the picture when I take it down! Help me, Lord! In slow motion, she laid the stocking on the dresser. Holding her breath, she reached across Erin's feet and inched the painting from the nail above the bed. She gently placed it on the carpet against the dresser and waited. Erin did not stir. Ever so carefully Heather lifted the stocking and hung it where the painting had been. Letting her breath out slowly, she stepped back.

She'll see it first thing when she wakes up!

It was almost midnight. Heather fell asleep on the sofa in the glow of the tree lights, listening to Christmas carols.

Giggles intruded into her dreams. Awaking slowly, she realized the giggles were coming from Erin's room. Springing up, she raced upstairs and into Erin's room.

"Merry Christmas!" Heather shouted. "We missed Christmas so we're having Christmas on New Year's."

"Oh, Mom." Erin laughed as she reached for her stocking. With a wide smile, she unwrapped and examined each small item, then hugged Heather.

"Thanks, Mom! You're silly, and I love you."

She thinks this is all there is, Heather gloated. *Wait till she sees the tree!* She hurried downstairs.

When Erin came down, Heather called to her from the living room.

"Erin, come here."

In the doorway Erin froze, taking it all in. The look of wonder on her face was worth all the effort and the late night.

"Oh, Mom, you must have stayed up until midnight!"

"I did!" Heather cried happily. "I had a wonderful time making Christmas for you! Because I love you."

"Oh, Mom, you're silly!" Erin hugged Heather again. "I love *you*!"

They had a wonderful Christmas. And it truly *was* Christmas. The magic was there. Because love was there. And that's really what Christmas is all about.

When Santa Came Early

During those gray November days, Rebecca felt that all of life had gone gray. She had discovered a painful lump that might be something serious. They struggled with finances. Fred's work boots leaked, soaking his feet with icy rain and snow. The tread on his hiking shoes was worn smooth, with a hole in one sole. And Fred seemed weighed down with a great sadness.

I'm worried about him, Rebecca admitted to herself.

He's probably afraid he's going to lose me, and wondering how he will pay all of the medical bills, she thought sadly.

Christmas would be bleak this year. Their elder daughter and her family had moved to Arizona the year before, and Rebecca and Fred had no hope of seeing them or their younger daughter, who lived in New Mexico. Rebecca knew that Fred felt alone and hopeless just as she did. Together they prayed and tried to trust, but their spirits did not lift.

One chilly day, Rebecca's brother Mark called. "I'm in New York State visiting my son Clark, and I would like to come Friday night and spend the weekend with you, if possible."

Rebecca was thrilled! Mark lived in Tennessee and had not stayed with them in at least twenty years. Since their apartment was tiny and the nights were above freezing, Rebecca made him a bed in their tent camper. She lent him a winter hat and piled the blankets up high. The small electric heater did not keep the chill away, but Mark seemed to love the adventure.

On Sunday, Mark drove them to the old stone church that he remembered from his college days. They took some photos, and on the way home Rebecca asked Mark to stop at Rota Spring Farm. She wanted to buy a few vegetables and give him a taste of Rota Spring's delicious ice cream. After she had picked up the produce, they lingered, looking around the store.

"I want to buy you a present," Mark told Rebecca. "Pick out something you want."

Oh, don't spend your money on a present for me, thought Rebecca. *All I really want is boots for Fred.*

On the other hand, I don't want to rob Mark of his joy in giving. Reluctantly she chose a pack of handmade greeting cards. They were cute and she would be able to use them.

Mark insisted on paying for the ice cream and asked if he could get whipped cream on his cone. The cheerful young lady behind the window responded affirmatively, and went on to list the items that came with the option of whipped cream.

"Chocolate fudge brownie sundae." Rebecca's mouth watered and her eyes crossed. She rarely ate sweets now, but years ago a dessert called Chocolate Fudge Brownie Delight had been her absolute favorite. Mark urged her to get whatever she wanted.

"I would like a chocolate fudge brownie sundae with one scoop of vanilla and one scoop of pumpkin Oreo® ice cream, with whipped cream, nuts, and a cherry on top, please."

What a scrumptious dessert! Rebecca enjoyed that sundae more than *anything* she had enjoyed in years. She managed to eat most of it, too!

"What else can I do for you?" Mark asked when they had finished the ice cream.

Do I dare ask? Timidly hoping, Rebecca spoke wistfully, "Fred really, *really* needs boots and shoes."

"Let's go," was Mark's immediate response.

As Fred chose boots and hiking shoes and Mark paid for them, tears of relief and joy flowed from Rebecca's eyes and would not stop. Then Fred showed her the loose, flapping soles on his old work boots. He kindly had not told her how bad they were so she would not feel worse than she already did.

They left the store and walked to Mark's car. "I want to take you out for pizza," Mark stated. "Where can we go?"

"Oh, boy, I'm hungry again," Rebecca chortled. "Let's go to The Trolley Stop. That's where we went when you and Dennis came on your motorcycles and took me for a ride," she reminded him. Mark bought pizza and Greek salad, both rare treats for Rebecca and Fred. They laughed and talked as they ate.

Warmed and glowing from the tangible love and generosity she and Fred had experienced, Rebecca threw her arms around her brother and squeezed him tightly.

"This day is the most fun I have had in a very long time. It was so good of you to spend time with us this weekend and get to know Fred a little. Thank you for everything. You have made me very happy." She smiled up into his loving eyes, hearing sleigh bells in her imagination.

True, Mark did not have a long white beard or a round belly that shook like a bowl full of jelly, but he was Santa nonetheless. The spirit of Christmas and of everything Santa stands for truly was embodied in this dear brother of hers. God *had* heard their prayers after all, and in His great love and compassion, He had sent Santa early.

The Best Christmas Gift

It was Christmas Eve. As she worked in the kitchen, Cathy could hear the girls in the living room enthusiastically playing house with their dolls. The sound of Bob's guitar from behind the closed bedroom door brought an ache to her heart.

Cathy patted the last red bow into place and surveyed her work. Five Christmas plates loaded with butter-cookie camels, gingerbread men, and green-sprinkled Christmas trees met her approving gaze. They made an island of beauty in a sea of flour, cookie sheets, and dirty dishes. Wearily, she glanced at the clock. No time to clean up the mess. She still had to deliver these cookies and get to the store before it closed, or there wouldn't be any special Christmas supper for her family.

Untying her apron, she carried all five plates of cookies to the living room, trying not to squash the bows. In the doorway she halted in dismay.

That room, too, was a disaster! Toys, books, and clothing cluttered the sofa and the braided rug that badly needed vacuuming.

"Oh, how did I go wrong?" she asked herself. "I've been working so hard all day—all week—and yet this Christmas I'm so far behind. Should I forget about delivering the cookies? No, I can't let our elderly friends go without some Christmas cheer. We're going."

"April, Jamie, put on your coats and mittens; it's time to go sing Christmas carols," Cathy called cheerily. No sense in dampening their Christmas spirit with her problems.

"Hurry! We'll have to clean this up when we get back."

Cathy knocked on the bedroom door. The guitar music stopped. Opening the door, she stuck her head inside.

"Bob, we're leaving now. Are you sure you don't want to come with us?"

"I'm sure."

"Okay. I'm sorry we left a mess. We'll clean it up when we get back."

Sadness gripped Cathy's heart as she followed the girls downstairs and strapped Jamie into her car seat. This would be the first Christmas Bob had not gone with them. There would be no guitar music and no deep voice to balance theirs as they sang to older friends in the community. No proud dad to watch his girls pass out the plates of Christmas cookies they had helped make and decorate. Tears welled up in Cathy's eyes as she thought of Bob's distance and coldness over the past few months. When not at work, he spent all his time in the bedroom playing the guitar. On rare occasions when he came out of the bedroom, he was cross with her, and even with the children at times. Cathy didn't know what was wrong. She didn't try to ask him about it anymore, because that just made him angrier. She and the girls were terribly lonely.

Cathy shook off the painful thoughts. "Look, girls, it's snowing!" she exclaimed. "Jingle bells! Jingle bells!" they sang as she drove in the gathering darkness through the falling flakes.

Cathy loved Christmas. Aside from the exhilarating cold, the sparkling snow, the pretty lights and decorations, there was a special something in the air. It seemed to her that heaven came a little closer to earth at Christmastime. People seemed kinder, more loving, more giving of themselves at this time of year, as though God's love, born in a manger, was born anew in their hearts. Her thoughts strayed to her favorite Christmas a couple of years before.

They had opened their few gifts before sunset on Christmas Eve, followed by caroling and a special supper. Close to 11:00 p.m., they roused the children from their beds and made their way to an antique box pew in the old church. There, warmed by woodstoves, they sang carols and heard the story of the miracle Baby in a manger. Later, after everyone was in bed, Cathy lay on the couch listening to Christmas records, enjoying the quiet beauty of the fragrant tree and the 1940s manger scene.

On Christmas Day two single friends had joined them after church for a delicious Christmas dinner. While the girls quietly played nearby, everyone lingered at the table discussing the amazing gift of love given by the Father. Toward sunset Bob took his guitar and they went caroling, giving out small loaves of cranberry orange bread. What a Christmas that had been! So restful, so full of love, giving, and gratefulness to God.

Will there ever again be a happy Christmas like that one? Cathy wiped her eyes as she stopped the car and they stepped out.

At each home they visited, the girls eagerly passed out a plate of Christmas cookies. Cathy's spirits lifted as she threw herself wholeheartedly into caroling and wishing "Happy Christmas!" to the recipients. The delighted looks on their faces were all the presents she needed that Christmas. And probably all she *would* receive, besides the girls' little homemade love gifts. She refused to let that diminish her spirits.

Afterward, Cathy stood hungry and exhausted in the tediously long line at the supermarket. The girls clung to her, whining. It was already past suppertime, and she still had to clean up the living room and kitchen before she could make supper. The girls would be cranky and difficult when she asked them to pick up their toys. They would probably fall asleep before they could enjoy traditional family time. And how enjoyable would Christmas Eve be with Bob hiding in the bedroom? Overwhelmed with fatigue and the dread of what faced her at home, Cathy just wanted to crawl between cool bedsheets and surrender to the oblivion of sleep.

Home at last, she dragged herself up the stairs to their second-floor apartment, carrying Jamie in one arm and the bag of groceries in the other.

Lord, help me! she pled silently. *I can't do this! Give me strength!*

She set Jamie down and shifted the heavy bag of groceries to her left arm to unlock the door to the apartment. The door swung open and April and Jamie ran inside. With a sigh, trying not to look, Cathy stepped through the door. Suddenly she stopped in bewilderment and shock.

I'm in the wrong apartment! No, the key worked, so it has to be right. In amazement, Cathy stared at the miracle before her.

The living room had been transformed! There was no trace of the chaos they had left behind. Christmas tree lights illuminated the bare floor and braided rug, which had been vacuumed. Soft candlelight shone on a Christmas tablecloth and a light supper of popcorn, fruit salad, and Christmas cookies. "Silent Night" played softly on the radio.

"Merry Christmas!" Bob shouted, appearing from the bedroom and grabbing her into his arms.

Cathy couldn't move. Tears brimmed in her eyes and spilled down her cheeks as the magnitude of what Bob had done dawned on her. Bob, who understood little about domestic chores, unselfishly had given of himself to make a new start at Christmas. He had given the gift of love.

> *Cathy couldn't move. Tears brimmed in her eyes and spilled down her cheeks as the magnitude of what Bob had done dawned on her.*

Suddenly Cathy realized Bob was waiting for a response. Throwing her arms around him, she laughed and cried hysterically with relief and happiness.

"I can't believe you did this! It's wonderful! Girls, look what Daddy did! Isn't it wonderful?"

Bob and Cathy grabbed the girls' hands and merrily danced around in circles. After a joyous meal, Bob got down on his hands and knees and gave the girls pony rides before they all sat snuggled on the sofa reading the story of Baby Jesus.

When the girls were in bed, Cathy rested in Bob's arms on the sofa in the glow of the tree lights.

"I'm sorry I don't have a gift for you," Bob whispered.

"You have given me the best gift I could ever dream of," Cathy murmured, and she nestled closer into his arms.

A Christmas to Remember

Julie turned the car into the parking lot. There was one more space, at the far end! She parked the car, turned off the engine, grabbed her purse and jumped out. Pushing the lock button on the car key, she dashed in her high heels across the parking lot and into the church. A man in a dark blue suit greeted her.

"I've come for the baptism," she said breathlessly. "Did I get here in time?"

"No worries," he replied. "The pastor is giving the sermon now, and then he will perform the baptism. Are you Hal's stepdaughter?"

A smile spread over her face. "Yes, I am," she answered.

"He has been waiting for you. He asked the pastor to hold off the baptism until you arrived. Go ahead inside; Hal is sitting on the left near the front."

Julie pushed open the swinging door and passed into the sanctuary. She drew in her breath at the beauty of the church decorated for Christmas. Evergreens adorned wide windowsills beneath honey-colored stained-glass windows. Slim red candles on golden candlesticks glowed from each cluster of evergreens. On the platform, a colorful crèche surrounded by red poinsettias and glimmering candles directed her thoughts to the meaning of Christmas, the real reason she was here today.

Julie's eyes scanned the worshippers. There he was! The back of his head was so familiar, even with white hair. Just then he turned around, his anxious eyes searching for her. His face lit up, and he gave her a little, unobtrusive wave. She hurried to squeeze in beside him. He put his arms around her and held her tightly. Her throat choked up and her eyes watered. How she loved him!

And today, of all days, she wanted to be here with him. How she had longed for this day! Sometimes, when she had heard the hardness, the bitterness, the sarcasm, in his voice, she had almost given up hope. But she had never stopped praying for him.

She knew her mother hadn't, either. How her mother would have loved to be here today! Julie knew how much her mother had longed for Hal to know and love Jesus, how the tears had come as she sat week after week in church without him by her side. Her mother would be so delighted when Jesus awoke her on resurrection day and she found Hal, with Julie, greeting her!

Julie stole a sideways glance at Hal. He sensed her looking at him, and his eyes met hers. His dear face seemed different—happier, maybe— more content. She patted his hand.

She was too excited to concentrate on the sermon. This was probably the happiest Christmas of her life! Julie recalled the first Christmas she had celebrated with Hal in the family. She was just seven years old. Life had taken on a new luster with Hal in it, and every Christmas had been special. Her own father never wrote or called, and Hal had become a father to her. He had taken her and Mom camping, showed them the USA on road trips, and taught her how to drive his pickup truck. Hal had been the one who attended her graduation, the one she had read her tribute to. He had bought her a used Toyota Camry for her graduation present. On the day she was married, it was Hal who had escorted her down the aisle and given her away.

Julie had finally succeeded in establishing fitful contact with her biological father, but Hal was the one who was really there for her. All of her life he had been there for her, although since tenth grade much of their relationship had been by phone calls and texting.

Tears stung her eyes. What was wrong with men, anyway? And women, for that matter. Why did they hurt their families? Just as her biological father had done, both of Julie's grandpas had wreaked havoc in their families. One, a loving Christian father, had left his wife and children, slicing through their hearts with a pain from which they had never fully recovered. Julie's maternal grandpa's drinking and carousing, and his verbal abuse and lack of religious faith and morals had left his children emotionally injured. Even Julie's father-in-law had left his family and moved out of state. All three men later in life apologized for hurting their children, but they could not turn back the clock to the way things had been, and the scars remained. And the list went on. Julie could name a handful of other men among her family and friends whose lives had demoralized their families.

When, in his old age, Grandpa Karl had invited Jesus into his life and been baptized, Julie and her mother rejoiced at the change in him. *But what about all the wasted years,* Julie wondered. *What about all the heartache my mother and her siblings suffered because of his lifestyle?* More than once her mom had said to her, with tears, "Why didn't my dad go to counseling and learn how to be a loving dad, or at least read books from the library? It wasn't his fault that he didn't know how to be a real dad, but why didn't he try to learn?" Another time she had told Julie, "One night, Grammie and I cried all the way home from prayer meeting after watching a film about an alcoholic who gave his life to Jesus when he heard his little girl praying for him. But my prayers for my dad didn't work." Neither had Julie's prayers for her own dad.

And what about the problem behaviors my mother and her siblings learned from their dad, and then had to unlearn as adults? What about the grandkids who suffered the lack of a loving grandpa, or had been negatively influenced by him? Julie had observed over and over that the way a father lives influences his children. His sons tend to grow up to be like him. His daughters tend to marry men like him. Immoral mindsets and behaviors, whether in the father or the mother, often are passed on to the children and grandchildren. And so the cycle of destruction continues.

When a man is almost ready for the grave and changes direction, how does that make up for, or undo, the wrongs he has done, Julie asked herself. *It doesn't, it can't,* she decided. *The toppled lives left behind him, the words he never said, the father he never was, cannot be made up for, by anyone. If only someone would tell young men this, before they come of age and marry.*

Oh, Lord, raise up the men! We need God-fearing men, true to duty, pure, noble, and loyal. The future of our families and of the world depends on them. Please, raise them up!

Mothers also influence and hurt their children, Julie knew from experience. Her own mother had made painful mistakes. But Julie was familiar with research showing that lasting change for the better in families begins with the father. He is the husband, the house-band that keeps the family together and guides it toward good, by example and by instruction.

A chill crawled up Julie's spine as she recalled how close she and her own husband had come to breaking the fragile thread of marriage after years of wounding each other and their children. Instead, together they had resolved to break the curse of divorce in the family. How glad she was that they had found a counselor at the Hope Restored program who had helped them heal from their wounds and learn how to communicate. He had shown them how to be unselfish servant leaders like Jesus. For selfishness is the true culprit, they had learned. Their boys thrived in the newfound happiness and stability of the family, and had matured into loving, loyal, and moral men. Their upright lives and strong marriages were a great satisfaction to her.

Hal shifted his position, and Julie gave him a smile. She was so thankful for him! Without him, she would have had no father. And Hal had been a good stepfather to her, even though he and her mother had not married. Hal had made life fun and interesting. He had never tried to take advantage of her body, as some fathers and stepfathers do. He loved all living things and was reluctant to kill even a black widow spider. He was an intelligent, faithful worker, always cleaning up after himself. He made his electronics wiring neat and beautiful, almost like an object of art, even if no one would see it. He saved his money, often generously giving to others in need. He loved to help people, and would probably give someone the shirt off his back, if needed.

In these things and more, he had been a great example to her. But the air seemed to turn gray on the rare occasions when his patience would at last become exhausted. His swearing had made her wince more than once. As a child, she had felt sick inside and had wanted to get away from him.

Sometimes Hal would mock her mother's religion, the religion he had been raised in. Seeing the hurt in her mother's eyes would bring a pang to Julie's heart. Julie had felt the sting of Hal's words as though they had been directed at her, because it was her religion, too. Already having been rejected by her father, she feared Hal would eventually reject her if she believed differently from him.

Why don't men realize how greatly their unbelief and lack of love for God wounds their families?

Julie shuddered. *Why am I thinking all of these negative thoughts on such a happy day?* She shifted her thoughts to the happiest period of her growing-up years. That had been when Hal was going to church with them regularly. As he attended church, his heart changed somehow—it had softened. The three of them became a united family, growing together in love for each other and for God. Julie had felt so secure. She still kept a copy of a letter Hal had written to the pastor, telling of his joy upon finding that the religion of his childhood finally made sense to him.

She and her mother had told Hal how much they enjoyed the change in him, from bitterness, hardheartedness and cynicism to the kind and respectful man he now was. Hal had recoiled in horror at their words.

"I was like that? Why did you stay with me?" he had asked, obviously disgusted with himself.

"Because we love you," they had assured him.

But they had moved to a different state, and Hal was not pleased with the new church and stopped attending with them. Julie heard the hardness come back into his voice whenever spiritual things were mentioned. That was when her mother had cried in church. Somehow the relationship deteriorated and Julie's mother moved far away, taking Julie with her.

Julie's body tensed, reliving the pain she had felt at losing him. Her eyes filled with tears. Hal gave her an inquiring look and rubbed her arm soothingly. She buried her face in his shoulder until she regained her composure. Hal stroked her hair. She sat up, gently blew her nose, and gave him a crooked smile to let him know she was all right.

Hal had called her regularly, and always made sure they had what they needed. On special occasions the three of them would get together and she pretended they were a family again, only to be ripped apart from him once more. She never could get enough of him, enough of his love, enough of his attention. She wanted him every day, not just a few days a year. And she still could not get enough of him, even now that she was an adult. She had lost out on half of her teen years with him, and could not seem to catch up. The ache never quite went away. It was always there, ready to surface whenever she allowed herself to think. She turned her head so Hal would not see her eyes watering again.

When they were together on Thanksgiving weekend of her senior year in high school, Hal finally mentioned the m-word to her mother. Julie waited with bated breath and leaping heart for her mother's response. For years she had longed for the commitment that would give her a stable home. At her mother's rather rude reply, all hope perished. Later her mother confessed to Julie that the thought of a lifetime with the loneliness and heartache of Hal being against religion had felt unbearable. All she had ever wanted since childhood was a happy Christian home. But they hadn't asked Julie what **she** wanted. Why couldn't they see what they were doing to her?

Julie got out a tissue and wiped her eyes. Hal put his arm around her and gave her a squeeze.

Why do families have to fall apart and move away from each other? Because of the disintegrations of her family, her boys had grown up without any grandpas to take them fishing. Her husband had missed out on both his dad's and Hal's friendship and mentoring. And Hal had become increasingly hard and bitter against religion.

Julie saw Hal a little more often now that she was married and lived in the West, but she wished he would spend more time with her. One Thanksgiving before her mother's death, Hal had lingered late at Julie's place, seemingly reluctant to leave them. That Thanksgiving she had wept after he left. How his bitterness hurt her! How badly she wanted him to know and love God! But it seemed like he was trying to pass on his unbelief to her. How she longed for the spiritual aspect in their relationship.

Why is it so hard for men to accept God and live by the principles of the Bible? Julie wondered. *Is it pride? Is it too difficult to submit to someone else and not be the boss of your own life? Is it because God is portrayed as a man, and many men have trouble forming close friendships with other men? Why do they?* Julie pondered that for a while. Then it struck her.

Perhaps it is because they have been deserted and injured by their own fathers. Why, that has to be at least part of it. Hal's father left his family when Hal was a teenager—the most vulnerable time of a boy's life, when he most needs his father. How devastated Hal must have been. His dad turned his back on religion and scoffed at his mother's beliefs. Hal must have been like a ship without a rudder. He lacked a father's moral and spiritual guidance at the very time he was trying to hammer out his own values, as his teachers were telling him in so many ways there is no God. And his sweet mother's honest efforts to serve God were misguided at best. Her rigid, extreme lifestyle and continual quoting from the Bible and religious books must have made both Hal and his father want to run screaming into the sunset. And my mother's failure to live up to her beliefs surely didn't help any. No wonder Hal did not find God!

Julie clicked her tongue in sudden sympathy. Hal raised his eyebrows and looked at her sideways with a quizzical face that made her snicker in spite of her serious thoughts. She knew Hal thought she was questioning something the pastor was saying.

Abruptly, the pastor's sermon ended, and he called Hal up onto the platform to publicly state his vows. Julie gave Hal a quick hug to steady him and whispered, "I love you." She knew how nervous he would be at getting up in front of everyone.

"I was raised in church," Hal began, with his eyes on Julie, "but I didn't want to become like the people I saw in church and in my own family. In public school, I was taught evolution as fact. I believed the scientists and the writers of the textbooks. I felt relieved to think that there was no God, and that I could live my life the way I wanted to instead of obeying some stupid rules that made people weird and looked down on by intellectuals.

"But instead of making me feel free and happy, trying to do without God and the principles of His Word often put me into struggles with my conscience and at odds with the people I loved. I felt that my parents had really messed me up.

"When I dated women who were raised in strict religions, I encouraged them to have a little fun instead of abiding by their beliefs. My relationships—and then my marriage—didn't last, and about the only things in my life were work and helping people.

"One day I decided to actually look at the evidence for a worldwide flood and creative design in nature and in the human body. What I found was astounding, and it convinced me that none of it could have happened by chance, even given millions of years. I found an amazing Creator, a true scientist whom I can admire.

"I found that every human cell is continually quantum computing!" Hal said with excitement.

Julie's face went blank. *What is he talking about?* Looking at her, Hal hesitated.

Continuing on in a calmer tone, he admitted, "Later, I studied the Bible with Dan, and found that this Creator not only predicts the future accurately, but that He loves me and gave His life for me."

Hal choked up. After several seconds, he managed to continue.

"When it dawned on me that I had spent a lifetime running away from and fighting an intelligent, wonderful person who loves me and died for me even when He knew I would reject Him, it broke my heart. This Creator is also a forgiver, and He has forgiven everything I have ever done that has hurt Him and others, and everything I should have done but neglected to do!"

Julie's eyes teared up as Hal told how Jesus had brought him understanding, and how he had found peace and happiness in surrendering to Him. Her heart overflowed with joy as Hal pledged his life to Jesus. After all these years, her prayers had been answered! How glad she was, even at this late date! She listened as the pastor explained that Hal's old life would be buried symbolically in the watery grave of baptism, and Hal would rise out of the water a new creation by the power of God. From now on, he would live for God, daily walking with Him and trusting in Jesus' continuing love and forgiveness.

Hal and the pastor departed to another room to change clothes for the baptism. As the organ played softly, a gentleman stepped up to the podium and opened his hymnal.

"Let's sing hymn number 318, 'Whiter than Snow,'" he announced. Julie turned to the correct page in the songbook, but her mind would not focus.

She had almost fainted when Hal had called her and invited her to his baptism. Then she became ecstatic! It was her mother's death that had made him think, Hal told her. Her mom had apologized to Hal. Looking back, she realized that many times she had been selfish, bullheaded, angry, and even cruel, and had held grudges. In spite of her verbal loyalty to God, she had hurt Hal with her words and with her actions, quite unlike the God she professed to follow. And Hal had forgiven her.

Julie knew her mom had gone to her grave believing that her former disregard of some of the principles of the Bible had kept Hal from seeing Jesus and wanting to know Him.

After she passed away, Hal had decided to see if there really was scientific evidence for creation and the flood that Julie's mom had believed in, which eventually led him to the Bible and to God.

Hal had seen too many Christians whose lives did not match their words, and he wanted none of that. Nor was he interested in a bunch of cold, powerless doctrines. He had searched until he found a man whose life showed that he truly knew and loved Jesus. Dan had helped Hal see Jesus and His love all through the Bible, and the Scriptures had come alive for him. Hal had seen that the Bible interprets itself, and that history, archaeology, and even science confirm the Biblical record.

A door opened into the baptistery. The pastor and Hal, in baptismal robes, descended a short stairway into the waist-high water. Hal had told Julie that he would much rather be baptized out in the river or the lake, but in December, at his age that would not be wise. Once he had made his decision, he did not want to waste any more time by waiting for warmer weather. He feared that if he did not act, his resolve would fade and he would grow hardhearted again.

Hal whispered to the pastor, and the pastor whispered back. Hal nodded, and the pastor called to her, "Julie, Hal would like you to stand at the top of the baptismal tank steps. Just come through the door on the left, and around."

While Julie approached the door, the pastor invited any remaining family and friends to watch on the platform at either side of the baptismal tank. Julie wondered which one was Dan.

Well, I'll meet him soon enough, and thank him with all my heart.

She reached her destination and gazed down into Hal's face, giving him a tremulous smile. Hal seemed confident, not nervous like she had thought he would be.

The pastor stood facing the audience, with Hal in front of him, facing Julie. Hal handed the pastor a folded white handkerchief. The pastor gripped it in his right hand and whispered to Hal to place his hands around the pastor's right forearm. Then the pastor raised his left hand toward heaven.

"Hal, because you have invited Jesus into your life, and because you love him and have pledged to follow Him with all your heart, I now baptize you in the name of the Father, and of the Son, and of the Holy Spirit."

The pastor placed the handkerchief over Hal's nose and mouth, and with his left hand on Hal's back laid him down under the water.

Water swished and streamed off Hal as the pastor quickly raised him to his feet again. Everyone clapped, and the pastor said, "Welcome to the family!"

Hal's face crumpled, and he made a beeline for Julie. Sloshing up the steps, he gathered her into his soaking embrace, and they sobbed in each other's arms. In the tightness of Hal's hug was apology for all the lost years. Undiluted forgiveness was in Julie's arms. Yes, she had missed out on her teen years with him. She had missed out on moral and spiritual guidance. She had missed out on the unity they would have had in Jesus. She wished this day could have come sooner. But Hal was here today. And she loved him. And that was really all that mattered now.

Because of Christmas, they would have eternity.

Friend, our heavenly Father understands and feels our emotional pain and hunger for loved ones who have been separated from us or have disappointed us. He has been separated from beloved family members ever since Adam and Eve in the Garden of Eden chose to believe Satan's lies about Him, rather than trusting His loving heart. For several thousand years He has gone to amazing lengths to reconcile us with Himself, because He longs to be with us. He wants us every day; He can never get enough of us. He yearns for you, for me, to spend time with Him, to know Him, to love and trust Him. Reluctant to shut the door of mercy, He waits a little longer before putting an end to sin and sinners, trying to draw us close to Him before it is too late. If we insist on living apart from Him, He will not force us. He will let us go. But through all eternity He will feel the pain of losing us, His precious, beloved family members.

Alight

As shepherds watched their sheep by night,
Suddenly into their sight
There burst an angel glowing white,
Who brightened up that dark midnight.

The shepherds huddled down with fright,
But soon their fear turned to delight.
"In Bethlehem is born this night
A Savior, who will make things right!"

The sky was set ablaze with light,
As angels sang with all their might,
"Glory to God up in the height,
And peace on earth," then took their flight.

The shepherds ran, no more uptight,
To see the Babe in manger site.
Above the stable, shining bright,
Hung angel star big as a kite.

Shepherds returned to flocks onsite,
But stopped to share and to invite
All people that they met that night,
While praising God! (so Luke did write)

And you, no matter what your plight,
Although you haven't been polite,
And sometimes even sin outright,
Are one of those whom God invites

To think about that starry night,
For there your love will re-ignite;
He is *your* Savior, your White Knight,
Who'll come and make your heart contrite.

Your best intentions He'll excite,
He'll flood your life with peace and light,
And bring you joy and great delight,
His friendship will be "out of sight!"

So please don't hesitate, sit tight,
And hurt the Savior, His love slight.
Don't be a sprite; just do what's right—
Give Him your heart this Christmas night.
Cathy Weaver, December 14, 2013

TEACH Services, Inc.
P U B L I S H I N G
www.TEACHServices.com • (800) 367-1844

We invite you to view the complete
selection of titles we publish at:
www.TEACHServices.com

We encourage you to write us
with your thoughts about this,
or any other book we publish at:
info@TEACHServices.com

TEACH Services' titles may be purchased in
bulk quantities for educational, fund-raising,
business, or promotional use.
bulksales@TEACHServices.com

Finally, if you are interested in seeing
your own book in print, please contact us at:
publishing@TEACHServices.com

We are happy to review your manuscript at no charge.

CPSIA information can be obtained
at www.ICGtesting.com
Printed in the USA
BVHW021048151222
654324BV00021B/106